An Angel Walked Beside Me

An Angel Walked Beside Me

Amazing true stories of children with special gifts

JOAN CHARLES

HarperElement
An Imprint of HarperCollins*Publishers*
77–85 Fulham Palace Road,
Hammersmith, London W6 8JB

www.harpercollins.co.uk

and *HarperElement* are trademarks of
HarperCollins*Publishers* Ltd

First published by HarperElement 2011

1 3 5 7 9 10 8 6 4 2

© Joan Charles 2011

Joan Charles asserts the moral right to be
identified as the author of this work

A catalogue record of this book
is available from the British Library

ISBN 978-0-00-742381-1

Printed and bound in Great Britain by
Clays Ltd, St Ives plc

The stories in this book are based on real incidents, but
names and some identifying features have been changed
to protect the privacy of the people concerned.

Mixed Sources
Product group from well-managed
forests and other controlled sources
www.fsc.org Cert no. SW-COC-001806
© 1996 Forest Stewardship Council

FSC is a non-profit international organisation established to promote the
responsible management of the world's forests. Products carrying the FSC
label are independently certified to assure consumers that they come
from forests that are managed to meet the social, economic and
ecological needs of present and future generations.

Find out more about HarperCollins and the environment at
www.harpercollins.co.uk/green

Dedication

I dedicate this book to all four of my amazing children who have been and continue to be my greatest teachers, my rocks. They give me endless amounts of encouragement and support; if it had not been for them continually saying, 'Go on, Mum – do it!' I might never have taken the first steps on this path which have led to such an amazing journey.

To my grandchildren, my little angels who continually surprise and delight me with their own simple yet amazing gifts.

To my mum and dad, who have passed from the Earth plane, but who gave me many spiritual gifts without realising how important they were.

To Rita, my sister, for giving me love, support and spiritual treasures along the way.

I couldn't forget my Uncle Joe, who was always my hero and who made my time with him very special.

A special thanks to Ellie and Colin for allowing me to write about their psychic talents and also to my daughters, Dannielle and Simonne, for their stories from when they were young which have helped to make this book possible.

To all the precious friends who have walked the path with me in times of challenge and adversity. They have supported me along the way no matter what. I want to name a few special ones: Maureen, whom I have known since my teenage years, who never judges, always listens and supports, and is constantly there for me; also Myra and Liz; my dear friend and spiritual mentor, Bill Whiland; Stephen and Jenny Cosh, who mean the world to me and continually support me and give sound advice; also my ex-husband Davy, who was truly instrumental in nudging me on my spiritual journey in the early years.

I feel blessed to have had such a wealth of love and support from family and friends. Words alone could never express the real gratitude and love I feel for you all.

I especially want this book to be for all parents and children who are on their own psychic journeys, in the hope that it provides a glimmer of hope, knowledge, support and understanding of the natural gifts with which we all arrived in this world, and that it allows you to take these gifts beyond all limitations on an incredible and amazing journey filled with magic.

Contents

Through a child's eyes

I first became aware of my psychic powers when I was five years old.

Actually, that's not true. I always knew I had those powers; I just didn't understand them.

When I was little, I always felt very alone, very isolated. I didn't know my place and I wasn't quite sure how to fit in. I was a shy child and constantly being told by my mother that I was 'highly strung'. What I really felt was that I had been invited to join a game but no one had told me the rules. I had a sense of there being something waiting for me, something that was my destiny, but, of course, I couldn't put it into words at such a young age. I always felt awkward, and I spent a lot of time sitting in corners, waiting, waiting, waiting – what was I waiting for? My life to start. My real life to start. The one in which everything made sense and the world stopped being such an unfathomable place. It would be a long time before that happened, but, when I was five, I got a glimpse of what I was waiting for and what was waiting for me.

Before I started school, my family – a very traditional, solid, working-class family – had moved from Port Glasgow in Scotland to Burnley, Lancashire. We lived in a house on the same street as my dad's brother, Uncle John, but I didn't have much to do with him. One night I was lying in bed. My little sister Rita was fast asleep in the bed next to me, but I was wide awake. It was dark, and my bed was positioned by the window. The curtains were open and I could see the moon shining high above me, but it wasn't comforting. I couldn't sleep because I had a terrible feeling of dread knotting my stomach and playing on my mind. I often had trouble sleeping, and this night was no different in that respect; however, none of the usual tricks did me any good. I counted sheep, I thought of nice things like my favourite dolly and I told myself that my mummy and daddy were in the room next door. The outside doors were locked and no one could get in. None of it made any difference, because something inside me knew that locks and doors couldn't keep everything out.

The sense of waiting – the waiting I always felt part of – was there, but I felt that it would soon be over.

As I lay in my bed, I saw what I still call 'the Dark Thing'.

Past the open curtains, a figure floated.

It took seconds but, to me, it felt like forever.

The Dark Thing was a terrifying winged shape and the name I gave it was automatic, but I also knew the name other people would use for it.

I was five years old and I had seen the Angel of Death.

Not only had I seen it; I had known, without doubt, what it was.

As it floated past, my heart was in my mouth and I felt terror coursing through my veins. When it had passed, I huddled under the bedclothes and a fleeting thought crossed my mind – *was it coming for me?* No sooner had the question been formed than I had my answer, an answer which came automatically from deep within me. *The Angel of Death wasn't for me; it was for my Uncle John.*

I must have fallen asleep eventually. The next morning, I knew that I would keep it a secret. My family didn't encourage openness, and I wouldn't have considered telling them for a second. This was something I had to keep to myself. I remember trying to convince myself that it had been a dream while knowing full well that it had been all too real to me. I had to deal with the memory of the terrifying Dark Thing, and also with my own sure knowledge that it had taken my Uncle John away.

As I've said, my family was not one in which children were encouraged to chat openly. It was very much a case of being seen but not heard, so when I went into the kitchen and found my mum and dad talking quietly I didn't interrupt.

I didn't reveal what I had seen.

I was quiet as a church mouse and sat on a kitchen chair waiting to be given my breakfast.

I was quiet as they talked in low voices.

I was quiet as my dad shook his head and my mum shed a tear.

I was quiet when I heard them say that my Uncle John had died suddenly the night before.

I was quiet, but I wondered why the Angel of Death had been shown to a five-year-old child and what on God's earth I was going to see next.

I have never told anyone this story before, but now, as I invite you into my world, it seems only right that I disclose this encounter. I have worked as a psychic medium for almost thirty years – and had the ability to see things for all of my life – but now I have decided to take the next step and share with you what I believe and what I have experienced. Given that I was a child who possessed psychic gifts, and given that some of my own children and grandchildren have also been blessed, I have never doubted the many tales I have heard or cases I have witnessed in which other children make contact with those they love, whether on this plane or on the other side.

I can only tell you what I have observed. It is up to you to make your own judgement about the journey on which I will take you in the pages of this book. I believe that every child – and therefore, every one of us – has the ability to communicate with spirit, and, when they pass, to retain contact with those they love who have been left behind. These whispers from another world can be heard if only we open our minds and souls to hearing them. The stories I will share with you are full of love and hope, yet the angels who act as messengers of tenderness and care are often dismissed, for in the world in which we live we are all too quick to reject the beauty in our lives.

At a time when so many of us are searching for meaning, I would encourage everyone to look at the natural and loving messages which surround us. They can add richness to our daily lives and relationships, giving us guidance and hope. We should cherish those who bring us such messages and listen to whispers from the angels who exist in all of our lives.

An Angel Walked Beside Me

Chapter 1

The stories that need to be told

I believe that all children possess psychic abilities, but that many are ignored, dismissed or even punished for voicing thoughts and feelings relating to the spirit world. I'm not suggesting for one moment that there are millions of children all over the world seeing the Angel of Death before they go to sleep at night, but I am suggesting there is an innate ability in most little ones to which we pay very little attention. This lack of attention prevents us from recognising something that we perhaps no longer understand but which could be of tremendous value to us if we simply opened our hearts and minds.

Many people reading this will be parents and I'd like you to pause for a moment and ask yourself some questions.

Has your child ever had an imaginary friend whom he or she is able to describe in so much detail that it sometimes stops you in your tracks?

Has your child ever been inconsolably afraid or inexplicably happy in a certain room or place for no apparent reason?

Have you ever visited somewhere your child has never been before only to find them unsettled or emotional or terrified, or experiencing some other inexplicable emotion?

Have they ever seemed sure that you have been to a place before when you absolutely know that this is their first visit? Does that seem odd to them? Do they take a while to believe you? There could be a reason for it, a reason as clear as day – they *don't* believe you, because this place seems so familiar that they can't believe it is new to them. And perhaps it isn't.

Have you heard your child laughing or talking when you, the sensible adult, know that there is no one else around? *Imagination*, you scoff again.

What about when your son or daughter tells you something about a long-gone relative, perhaps a beloved grandparent of yours that they couldn't possibly know? Do you dismiss that as a comment you must have made to them about that person without remembering it?

What if they point to someone in a photograph, some-one who died long before they were born, and tell you something uncannily accurate about that person? Imagi-nation again?

How many reasons – how many *excuses* – can you keep providing before you have to face up to what is staring us all in the face?

Let's consider something radical.

Maybe children *aren't* making it all up.

Perhaps they do see, hear, smell and sense spirits in a way that makes grown-ups uncomfortable, but which seems perfectly natural to them. Whether you believe that or not, I would like to take the opportunity within this book to tell you about some of my experiences with children.

I can fully understand why some people are sceptical. When I saw the Angel of Death from my bedroom window, I would have loved it if someone had managed to explain it away. I wanted to be 'normal', I wanted to fit in. Perhaps there was a defiance in me that prevented me from accepting any so-called 'rational' explanations (and I now feel blessed that this was the case), but the terror I felt in those early years was not something I would wish on anyone.

The vast majority of children I have encountered have only happy experiences of the spirit world, whether they are the ones receiving or sending the messages, and I hope this will offer comfort to grown-ups who have lost touch with those abilities in them-selves. Opening yourself up (through recognising your own talents or those of the children around you) will not invite terrible things into your life. The experiences I have had are, by far, ones of hope and love – and surely only a fool would reject having more of those blessings in their lives.

The journey I will take you on in this book will be one in which I share the many encounters I have had throughout the years, encounters which have been both beautiful and touching. To get to this stage of my life, I have had to face many challenges, but all of them have been for a reason. During my childhood there were times when I had no control over what was happening, over which spirits were coming through. I wasn't seeking these experiences, and I wasn't revelling in them, but they happened anyway. From the age of seven, I knew, every time I looked in the mirror, that I was looking at someone who was here for a purpose. This was terrifying to me. I was only a little girl and I had no idea what this knowledge meant. Why was I thinking that way when I should have been concerned with nothing more complex than playing with other children? The feelings were so strong and they came at such a young age that they scared me. On reflection, as an adult I know that it was my intuition guiding me to the place I am now, but I don't want anyone to think that I was so egotistical I believed I was more 'special' than anyone else. I think everyone has a purpose, but we don't all recognise it.

By the age of eight or nine, it was obvious that school simply didn't grab my attention. I spent a lot of time daydreaming, looking out of windows, gazing into space. I had my own inner visions and heard an inner voice as naturally as other children played hopscotch. I dreamed of the day when I would finally be happy and feel 'normal' – whatever that was. I wanted to fit in. That would be my paradise. I longed for a time when I would no longer feel like a stray piece of jigsaw in the wrong box. My inner voice told me that everything would be all right and that things would work out, but in reality I was in a world that didn't seem to have a place for me.

I had friends, but often in the middle of playing with them I would finish what they had been about to say. On one occasion I was with a friend who had a dog. She began to talk, and I immediately interrupted to say that I knew her dog had died the night before. She was surprised, and wondered how I knew – but I just knew things. I was always so highly strung and nervous that every little thing worried me. Looking back as an adult, I can see that this was because I felt too much, I sensed too much around me, and I couldn't put any of it into words.

I always knew when things weren't going well between Mum and Dad. I didn't need to overhear arguments to realise that this was the case. I would lie in bed listening and, if I felt things weren't right, I would go downstairs and sit near by as I felt that my presence would calm things down. They never told me to go back to bed, so maybe they realised I was helping.

When I was seventeen, I met Davy, my husband-to-be. I loved him so much and knew that he loved me. He was my twin flame, my true connection, and I was very happy, but at the same time something inside me knew it would never last and that we would part. We were so much in love that this seemed a crazy thought, but it haunted me every day we were together. I was right – we did separate; but I have a lot to thank him for as everything that happened in our relationship moved me towards being the person I am today.

My life has been an amazing journey and it's still far from over. I'll tell you a little more about how I work as we travel this journey together. One thing that has become clear to me over the years of living and working as a psychic is that we are currently living in a moment when the importance of children with special gifts will become more and more obvious, and I want to share some of my stories with you to explain the ways in which these can manifest themselves. It's not easy being a psychic child. This is something I know from personal experience.

Learning to communicate with spirit

When the gift is in its early stages, in other words when the psychic is a child, there are few boundaries. They can end up fending off countless spirits all jostling for attention every minute of every day. I sometimes imagine the spirit world as a frantically busy place whenever a new 'route' for sending messages appears. They all have so much to say and they all desperately want their loved ones to know that they are fine, so the appearance of a child who can pass on their messages gives them a means of being heard. When I was little, I had no way of making sure that I was the one choosing when and what to hear – and some spirits take advantage of that. Most spirits are well-meaning, but it would still be a draining life if day after day allowed no respite from the barrage of messages being sent through.

As I got older and more comfortable with my gift, I learned more about how to be selective. At times, that involves me being strict about when I'll accept messages, or it can mean that I block some senders – it's a bit like having psychic email. Now I only pick up my messages during work hours if possible, I ignore the junk mail, and there are certain senders whom I never encourage.

However, there are still times when it is open season. If I'm preparing for a show, for example, I have to take the firewall down for the day and see who comes through. On such days I get a lot of communication. Sometimes I will sense someone walking beside me, or I will receive a direct message in my head that is clear and precise, like an order. Sometimes I will feel an emotion that I know is coming from someone else, or I will smell something very distinct. It may be that none of it makes sense at that moment, but I know that during the show these will be clues I need to pass on to others. Spirits can use a scent or a name or a place or a feeling to connect with those they have left behind. They will send me messages to prove that what I am saying is genuine, and, to me, this is crucial. I always prove things. Whenever and wherever I can, I will give people incontrovertible evidence by relating facts that I couldn't possibly know. Once people have been reassured about the genuine nature of my gift, I can move on to the real point which needs to be passed on. Some mediums feel they shouldn't have to provide proof, but it has always been an integral part of the way I work.

Throughout my psychic development I have had the gifts of clairvoyance, clairsentience and clairaudience. The earliest example of clairvoyance was when I saw the Angel of Death at the age of five. As I got older I felt as if I was watching a TV screen in my mind's eye, one that was as real as anything else around me. When I imagined myself older and happy, I was experiencing 'precognitive clairvoyance', which meant I was seeing myself in the future through a vision.

I always had clairsentience. I felt things even though I often couldn't explain why I felt them. I could sense or feel when someone was not right in themselves because I would feel it in me too. If someone felt sick, I would feel sick too. I still have that gift very strongly.

Clairaudience came much later in life when I had been developing and working as a psychic for some time.

I could always see and feel, but it was a while before I heard anything much. I started to hear a name here and there, and it was as if spirits were allowing me to build this gift slowly so that I could cope. It developed over time and now I hear spirit speak to me internally as a matter of course.

Sometimes one of my gifts works more strongly than another – I just go with whatever comes along and trust that it will all be fine, and this has generally worked very well for me.

On top of these gifts, I have always had the ability to read auras. When I began going to spiritualist churches, giving readings and working as a psychic, auras became more and more clear to me. When I was in my early thirties, I studied aromatherapy and found that the more I worked with people, the more connected I became. I would see flickers of light around them, and sense spirit. As I progressed, I saw changing colours and shapes as well. This is how auras work; they change according to what is happening in the individual's life at any given time.

There are seven main layers in an aura. The first is a kind of smoky haze, rather like what you would see if you were driving along on a summer's day after it had been raining. When the sun comes out, the haze begins to rise, and this is very similar to that first, or etheric, layer of an aura.

The second layer is the emotional layer, which has colour. It begins to expand out of the body, and this is where connections are made.

Level three is the mental layer, the one that relates to how we process the intellect or thought. Basically, it is about what makes us tick and it also relates to the way in which things worry us to a greater or lesser degree. When a psychic taps into this layer, they will be able to see, sense or experience how the person copes with things in their life at a practical or logical level.

Level four is the layer referred to as the astral layer. It is the bridge that crosses between the third and fifth layers. The first three are all linked to the physical world of the individual and the way in which they manage in it, but as you cross the fourth you enter into a more spiritual realm of love and greater consciousness. It is rather like a portal between the first three and final three layers.

The fifth level is the etheric template. This layer is a copy of the previous layers, but one that taps into a greater consciousness. It is where physical and spiritual thoughts merge and can become manifestations through focus, love and vibration. A manifestation is when you think about something and focus your attention on it and it happens. It is where anything is possible if we focus on it.

Level six is the celestial layer. It connects with dreams, intuition and greater knowledge. It is turned on through meditation and other spiritual practices that enable mediums to work in these realms.

Level seven is the ketheric layer. This is like a shell that holds all the other auric layers in place. It contains all knowledge and understanding of everything you have ever done, a map of where you have been and what you have done and where you are heading. Very few of us get more than small glimpses of this layer, but I sometimes see it when a person has been reincarnated.

Like most professional mediums, I often take part in shows and tours. The sheer number of people at these events, both in the audience and in spirit, is staggering, but I firmly believe that if a message needs to come through, it will. Those who have passed over have such love for those of us who remain behind on the Earth plane that they keep trying until they finally make contact. Relationships are not ended simply by the passing of one party; they do not fade away because one person is no longer visible to the other.

When I am working at a show I need to use all my gifts to bring messages to the person whom they concern. I will be reading auras, hearing messages, seeing images, feeling emotions and sometimes smelling scents as well, and I have to put together all these signals in order to communicate them to the member of the audience for whom they are intended. I'm going to finish this first chapter with a story that demonstrates the way this can work in practice.

Ben and Hannah

As I stood on the stage at an event one night, I began to receive very strong messages about a young man called Ben. He was only eighteen years old when he had passed. Sometimes a person can pass at a very young age without there being a sense of sadness or pain because they have shut down as a coping mechanism, but with Ben I knew his passing had been traumatic. My body ached as soon as I was connected to him. It was very clear to me immediately from the sensations and imagery I was sent that Ben had been murdered in a completely senseless act. This obviously meant that it was going to be a very difficult communication that would have to be handled sensitively. In order for me to 'prove' the truth of the message, I would have to pass on some upsetting information.

'I have a message here for Ben's mum,' I began. A lot of people raised their hands, as it is quite a popular name, but I knew that soon there would only be one woman left. 'This is hard, and I know it will bring up some bad memories, but I really need Ben's mum to remember why she's here tonight. You want to know that he's okay – and we both know why that matters so very much to you, don't we?'

Any mother in the audience who had lost a child would want to know whether they were all right in spirit, but I hoped that my words would strike a particular chord with this woman. There were lots of murmurings, as there always are, and then one lady in a row not too far from the front caught my attention. She had lowered her arm but she had never taken her eyes from my face. She was shaking and tears were falling silently down her cheeks.

Despite the fact that I was wearing a microphone, my words were quiet. 'You know who you are, don't you? And you know why I'm going to have to say these words. Ben was only eighteen when he was taken from you and it was in a terrible way, wasn't it?'

Even though I was on stage, I could clearly see the woman shaking. I wished I could go down and hug her, but I also knew that if she stayed with me through this I would be able to bring her comfort that would last forever.

'He was murdered, wasn't he? Your beautiful boy was murdered.'

The woman nodded through her tears and the rest of the audience turned towards her. I needed to make sure she knew this wasn't entertainment, that this was real. I needed to prove it to her.

'I know that this hurts,' I said, 'but if I tell you what I know, what I couldn't possibly know unless I was being sent it, will that help you to understand that I really do have a message for you?'

The poor woman kept nodding and I could feel her pain. 'This month, September, is important for you because that's the anniversary of his death. Am I right?'

Again, she nodded.

'There were two people involved, I can see that. One of them was less connected than the other, but she did nothing to help, which is why I'm saying two people. I also know that it was to do with money. Your son wasn't involved in what they were up to, but he was in the wrong place at the wrong time, wasn't he?'

All through this, the woman wept, but I needed to go on.

'It was a brutal and unprovoked attack, it was at night, and it was in a dark place. I'm getting somewhere that looks like a very quiet area. Ben was taken by surprise and it was all over in a flash. I know that his killers were caught, but you think they got off lightly. I also know that you know the family of one of them and that you still have to see and be around these people.'

All of this must have been very hard for the poor woman to listen to, but I had to press on and get to what she needed to hear.

'You're right,' she finally said. 'It's all true. I don't know how you know all of that, but you're right. Thank you.' She started wiping her tears away.

'That's not all!' I said. 'What I've just told you is just my way of proving that what's coming next is genuine.

Ben is fine, he's come to terms with what happened and he wants you to reach that place of peace and forgiveness too. He knows that this has been awful for you – not just losing him, not just the trial, but the way in which you've had to keep seeing his killer's family. But he's being looked after now. That's what I have to let you know.'

She looked up at me with such hope in her eyes. 'Has he told you this? Is he telling you this now? Is he here?'

'No, no, he isn't here – but the person who is looking after him is.'

'What do you mean?' she asked.

'Hannah,' I told her. 'It's Hannah. I got all of this from Hannah, and she wants you to know that Ben is happy. He's with her and has been from the moment he passed. She loves him and she'll always care for him until you are joined together again. You know who I mean by Hannah, don't you?'

'Yes,' she whispered. 'Of course I do. I remember her so clearly. I always wished she'd been here to see Ben, and when he was born I missed her presence so much.'

'There was no need,' I told her. 'She was there. She's always been there. And now she has Ben to look after. She's your big sister, isn't she?'

The woman was in floods of tears again, but I could tell that she wasn't upset in the same way as she had been earlier.

'Hannah passed to spirit when she was eight, didn't she?' Again, her nods told me I was right. 'Her job when she was here was to look after you; she was a proper big sister and loved that responsibility. That hasn't changed. When Ben joined her, she made it her job to look after him. She's with him all the time and both of them are with you. Ben is safe now – and so is Hannah.'

It was a communication full of love and light. Hannah came across as very playful but also as someone who had welcomed the opportunity to take on responsibility when Ben passed over. I knew that she had died suddenly, from a viral infection, and felt that this was a link she had with the boy. Both of their passings had been unexpected, but she was in a stronger place to help Ben come to terms with his own situation. I could tell she was a delightful child, because I was getting very playful energy from her, but the energy she sent me from Ben was not the same. He was much quieter and more reflective. She channelled the information from both of them to me in order that I could pass it on.

When I work with someone, I always get a feeling of them, a sense. It's my inner voice. Clairvoyance, clairsentience and clairaudience are all working together, but usually 'the sight' is stronger than the others. It's like a movie running in my head, and I tend to chatter away as if I'm staring into space. I'm watching it all and reporting it back – and I have a library of these files and people in my head. I can access that library, those files, whenever I want. The deeper I can dig into those files, the more bizarre the proof I can uncover. There's no point asking 'Do you know a John?' because everyone does! I need to find specific and particular proof – for example, there was one case where I asked a woman about her sister and could tell her that she was obsessed with monkeys. After hearing the proof, they are ready for the message – and if it comes from someone called 'John', so be it!

With Hannah, I kept seeing a smiley face and I heard her saying, 'I'm okay, I'm okay, I'm fine.' She wanted me to pass on a message of reassurance, and she was reassuring me as well. Anything to do with children who have passed over is emotional for me. It is upsetting to think of a child who has been in pain or who has experienced suffering. Hannah's spirit was a beautiful one, and it showed not only in her concern for Ben and her family, but also in that which she showed to me. She had been ill for over a year, and things had got progressively worse. To have a child communicate that information while still saying 'I'm fine' was very touching. Hannah's essence was very strong.

Essence comes over to me a lot. The essence of the person goes beyond their physical form. Your body is just a vehicle to get you through this journey. I always look at it this way. Say you're going to see family in Australia. You might travel from anywhere in the country to get to

London for the first stage of your journey, then you'll probably take a connecting flight, maybe in Singapore. That's similar to what your soul will go through. Your journey will be broken up into lots of bits, all leading towards a final destination, all connecting with each other. Each piece of the journey is about what you're going to learn, what will build your soul and energy and knowledge so that the next time you come to this plane you will know things or be able to pick up something you left off.

Ben's essence was different from Hannah's. He was a quiet, introverted boy, who just went about his own business. I could see that he only had one or two friends, and tended to keep himself to himself.

Ben's mum was surprised to hear that he was with Hannah. 'But Hannah was dead before my son was even born!' she said.

It's true they hadn't known each other in this world, but in spirit you are part of a connected consciousness and, as such, constantly aware of your family members. We leave the physical body behind and go back to the energetic body which connects us all. There is no separateness in this state. It doesn't matter whether you believe in God or any other deity; we are all part of a universal energy. When your soul passes on, when it goes home, you connect back to your universal family. It's beyond religion; it has nothing to do with our narrow conceptions of how best to believe. Hannah watched Ben for years, and when he passed she knew as much about him as his own mother. In fact, had she been here on Earth she would probably have known less!

On this plane we are so focused on life and death that we often fail to see the continuity that exists. People, spirits, souls don't simply disappear. I believe that all children have an ability to make connections with the spirit world, and I also believe that those spirits who have passed during childhood have a special warmth and innocence that makes their love so special to those they left behind. They show it in many ways, as Hannah did by caring for her sister's son, and if we all unlock our minds and move past our worries we will see that someone's passing is an opportunity to open ourselves up to love that never ends – a love which children understand perfectly.

I believe that all children are psychic and that we as adults have a responsibility to nurture and encourage these gifts. As I share the wonderful stories in this book with you, I hope you feel the presence of these angels who walk beside us, and I hope you can find it in your heart to help whatever children there may be in your world to find their own spiritual and angelic path.

Chapter 2

The journey of life

When I am communicating with a child in spirit, a feeling of playfulness often comes through, which is a lovely thing to experience. In some cases the messages I receive are from a very early stage of life when I can sense a child waiting to be conceived. This might sound odd, but let me explain. When we are souls on a higher plane, we make decisions about whether we want to reincarnate and, if so, which parents we will choose. I'll explain more about this later, but when a soul is waiting to be conceived by a particular couple I can often sense them waiting. On many occasions I've predicted pregnancies, and this can be a very emotional experience for me as well as for the person for whom I'm doing the reading.

I need to handle my answers with great delicacy when a woman asks, 'Am I going to have a baby?' I can see some things, but I'm not an obstetrician or gynaecologist. Maybe I will see a baby but can't predict exactly when it will come. A woman's emotional need for a baby can cloud matters, so that her own body may not even know what's going on. Any medium who comes out with a definitive 'yes' or 'no' answer is really putting their head on the chopping block. But, having said that, I've done it many times.

At a reading, I may not know how long a woman has been trying to get pregnant, what doctors have told her or how fraught the whole subject is for her. This is one of the most difficult types of readings to do. The mere fact that a woman asks me if she will have children doesn't necessarily mean that she wants them. I would never assume that the question meant that she was desperate to become a mother, or indeed that she had no children already.

Sometimes you have to make a snap decision about whether to tell a woman what you see for her. I might inch my way towards it. I remember reading for one lady and I asked her, 'Do you see yourself having kids?' She said that she did, and I followed up by enquiring whether she fancied having quite a few. It was a relief when she said 'yes' to that as well. 'You better prepare yourself,' I told her, 'because you're going to have six!' This would have been shocking news for some, but she said that was the number she had always pictured herself with. I think we often know what's in our future if we listen to our own inner instincts.

When a woman called Fiona came for a reading, I could see immediately that she desperately wanted to have a child and that this was the main question she was planning to ask me; in fact, it seemed to be the whole purpose of the reading. Almost before she sat down she had asked, 'Will I have a child?'

There was no doubt in my mind. 'I absolutely feel there is a child waiting here for you, in spirit,' I told her. 'The child's energy is a little boy.'

Fiona started to cry. 'But the doctors have told me that I can never have children.'

'I'm not medically trained,' I replied, 'but I'm sorry – I don't care what they've said. I can only tell you what I feel and what I can see. I wouldn't say this if I thought it wasn't the case. I could never be that cruel.' I paused, then asked her a very important question. 'Don't you feel this is your destiny too?'

'Yes!' she cried. 'I absolutely do and always have. I've always wanted to have children but have never been pregnant. I've been for tests and specialists have said it will never happen. It breaks my heart to think of a future without a child in it.'

'There's something stopping it from happening at the moment,' I told her. 'But you need to know that what the doctors are saying is nonsense because there's a little boy waiting for you. Go and get him.'

It would have been completely wrong of me, both professionally and morally, to give her false hope. If the doctors were right, I was now setting Fiona up for even more heartache, but I truly believed that she would live her dream and that she would have a baby one day. If I had had even the slightest doubt of that I would never have told her what I did.

Fiona was shaking her head. She desperately wanted to believe what I was saying, but she had also had many years of hope crushed by disappointment and was wary of letting herself be optimistic again. I needed to make her believe that her negativity could be the very block that was preventing her from conceiving in the first place.

'I can see him, Fiona,' I continued. 'I can see your little boy – he's a cute wee thing, an old soul, and very intuitive. Don't worry; it will happen because this baby is just sitting there waiting. In fact I can see twins waiting for you.'

It was a difficult moment because I didn't want to push this poor woman too far. I left her to think about the message and continued with the rest of the reading, knowing that I had to wait and see whether Fiona would take up what I had said. There was a child waiting in the wings for her. Once she was in the correct emotional state and the divine timing was right, the baby would come.

About four years later I had an appointment to do a reading at what I thought was a new client's house. I had a vague recollection of the woman who opened the door but couldn't quite place her. I always recognise a face but am not always sure where from because I meet so many people in my work.

'Do you remember me?' the woman asked immediately. 'My name's Fiona. You told me I'd have twin boys, when every doctor I'd ever seen said it was impossible.' She smiled at me. 'Look,' she whispered. She pushed the door wide and a wee laddie of about four ran towards us. 'That's one of them,' said Fiona. 'That's Archie, one of the babies you saw, the one you said was waiting in the wings.'

As I watched this little miracle throw himself into Fiona's arms, I could have burst into tears. He was a beautiful little blond child and I could see in his eyes that, as I had predicted, he had been here before.

'I got pregnant a few months after you did my last reading,' she told me. 'I was amazed. I knew this must be the miracle babies that you had seen for me, but I could still hardly believe it. The doctors couldn't believe it either, but they couldn't dispute what was happening. I sailed through the pregnancy and they're the most perfect boys you could imagine. They're all I've ever wanted and everything you said they would be.'

It was lovely to be able to be part of that joyful story. I get goose bumps just thinking about it. How many other women have been told that they can't have children or that they've missed their chance, so they stop trying, whereas if they just left it to divine timing they might find that a miracle happened? I'm not saying that medical advice is always wrong. Of course there are many couples who suffer infertility for genuine physical reasons, but I think that for some people there are mental blocks in the way of conception. The power of the mind can work both ways.

Archie and his twin brother James were the children who were meant for Fiona and I knew she wouldn't have any more. When you are on the next plane you make decisions about your own journey. It's a strange combination of free will and 'what will be will be'. I believe that we choose our parents for a reason. I know that I chose my parents, siblings and even friends to allow me to develop my gifts. Sometimes those choices will bring bad things to us, but we need to come through a learning curve. Once we are on the Earth plane we have free will and can adapt those choices as we learn.

Joanne's blue eyed girl

When Joanne came to me for a reading, she had been having a lot of emotional issues with her family. Her mother had died and her brother was very unwell with stress, and on top of this she desperately wanted a child. It was the first thing which struck me about her, and the first thing I brought up, as it was clearly so important to her.

'You really want a baby, don't you?'

She nodded and the tears welled up in her eyes immediately.

'I can see that you've been trying for a while now, but had no luck.' Actually, I could see that it was becoming an obsession with her. I also knew that it was nothing to do with luck; babies come when they are needed and when the soul you require in your life is ready to be with you, but I had to be sensitive about what I said.

'It's all I think about,' she confided. 'I can't help it. I spend all my time wondering why I'm not pregnant, or dreaming of holding my own child. I look at baby clothes, plan the nursery, think of names. I chart my menstrual cycle, work out the best times to try, eat healthy things, do all I can – but nothing. I fear it's never going to happen,' she wept. 'I fear I'm never going to be a mum.'

I could see that Joanne was perfectly healthy. She hadn't lost babies, she hadn't miscarried. I knew exactly what was happening, but I also knew that what I was about to say would frighten some people.

I took her hands in mine and looked into her eyes. 'Everything will be fine,' I told her. 'I need you to listen to me and I need you to believe this: your baby is there. Your baby is waiting for you and, when the time is right, your baby will come.'

'Can you see it?' she asked. 'Can you see my baby?'

'Yes, I can. There's a little girl waiting to arrive, but she won't come until the time is right – and the time is *not* right at the moment. She has the most striking blue eyes; they're piercing and will take your breath away when you see them. This is important: when she arrives, she will be a very particular sort of child. She will know when things are going to happen. People will say she's an "old soul" or that she has an "old head on young shoulders", and they'll be right. Your daughter will be born wise. You'll see.'

'Really?' she asked. 'You can see all of that?'

'As clear as day. But there's something else. There's a reason your girl isn't here yet. The timing has to be perfect. This baby who is waiting for you to become her mother is actually your spirit guide so she has another purpose at the moment.'

Joanne looked puzzled. 'What do you mean?'

I explained that a spirit guide is someone who guides us in life. It is often someone we know who has passed over, but not necessarily, and your guide can change at different points in your life depending on your needs. I continued: 'You are going through so much emotional trauma that you need your baby's energy as support. The loss of your mother and the worry about your brother are such a heavy load to carry that she knows you wouldn't be up to a pregnancy as well. She needs you to be in a much better place before she arrives. As soon as you stop worrying, you *will* conceive. Your baby is with you already, helping you. Let nature take its course and she will be here with you on this plane before you know it.'

It was as if a cloud had lifted from over Joanne. Her face changed. She looked bright and alive, a million miles away from the way she had been when she arrived.

Almost two years later I was walking in my local high street one Saturday when who should I bump into but Joanne and her brother – and Joanne was pushing a pram. Inside, fast asleep, was a gorgeous little girl of just under a year. She opened her eyes as I peeked at her and I saw they were a startling azure blue. I felt as if she was looking into my soul. I also felt as if I knew her.

Joanne said that she felt the same way. 'I don't feel as though she's only been with me for ten months,' she said. 'I feel as if she knows everything about me and that we've met before.'

I laughed. 'That's exactly the case! She *has* been here before and she has known you forever.'

She was glowing as she walked away – and I was excited too because I know I am going to hear a lot more about that child over the years.

Babies in waiting

There have been many instances over the years when I've predicted a pregnancy or twin babies – too many to mention, as that is such an important part of many women's lives. Women in their fertile years often come for readings simply because they feel more in tune with their spirituality. It is the child that I sense; there is a feeling of waiting energy or an energy that is already present. Sometimes I've known that a woman is pregnant before she knew it herself, because the energy of the baby is already there.

Once I was getting ready to do a reading at a young woman's house when I noticed a little ornament in the corner. It was a man and woman embracing, but the centre was open and I immediately knew, by glancing at it, that she was going to have a baby. As usual, I had to be careful about broaching the subject so I asked a general question: 'Are you broody?' When she said that she was, I told her that she wouldn't have long to wait!

Sometimes when a person is in a new relationship there's a different energy about them; their aura changes colour. Auras also change colour when a woman is pregnant because there is an energy that shines through them. Sometimes this can be confusing for mediums, and we need to take our time to work out whether it is one thing or the other. When a baby is actually there, no matter how soon after conception, there is an excitement about the woman's aura, a real feeling that this is happening.

Children who are in tune with their psychic talents are likely to pick up on babies-in-waiting. One woman I read for told me that her five-year-old son had come in from school with a beautiful card, which he had made for her. On the card was an angel. She told him it was lovely and asked what it was for.

'It's to welcome the new baby,' he told her.

'I'm not having a baby!' she answered.

'Yes, you are,' he said. 'There's a baby in your tummy.'

The mum just put it down to wishful thinking, but he continued: 'It's my birthday present – you'll have the baby for my birthday.'

She tried to put it out of her mind, but it niggled at her for a few days until she gave in and bought a pregnancy testing kit. The test was positive – and at her first antenatal appointment the obstetrician confirmed that the baby was indeed due on her first son's birthday. That little boy had been showing quite a few signs of psychic awareness, but this was something so concrete that everyone was amazed.

My own family

As a mum and a granny myself, I've had plenty of experience of pregnancies and babies. When my own four children were born, I was still young and didn't have the confidence in my abilities that I have now so I was never able to see anything very clearly, but with the pregnancies of one of my daughters I really had to hold my tongue so that I didn't let the cat out of the bag. When my daughter Dannielle was expecting her first wee one, I knew from the outset that she was having a little girl – I could see her waiting. Dannielle, on the other hand, was certain that she was going to have a boy. I told her that a scan was a waste of time as she had a mother who could see just as well as any machine. Nevertheless she went ahead and there was no surprise for me when she called to say that my first granddaughter was on her way. It happened in her next pregnancy as well, when I told her she was having a boy; she still thought she was having a girl until she found out that once again I knew best.

I try not to overuse my psychic abilities where my own family is concerned, but there was one day during Dannielle's first pregnancy when I felt terribly unsettled. I was waiting for her to visit and I felt a huge uneasiness, a sense that something just wasn't right. I became more and more frantic but was unable to see exactly what was wrong. I felt sick to my stomach. When Dannielle finally arrived, she was also upset and shaken as it turned out that she had fallen quite badly. She had been checked over by a doctor and the baby was fine, but it did make me reflect on the difficulties that are thrown up when I can only see part of the picture. I hadn't known exactly what had happened, or that she would be all right; I only knew that something was amiss, which is scary when it concerns a member of your own family.

My children would sometimes complain about the way my gifts affected them. After one of my sons passed his driving test, he was keen to be out and about in the car as much as possible, despite having little experience. He didn't have a car of his own and when I lent him mine it was with conditions attached, the main one being to avoid a notorious road near where we lived which was an accident blackspot. He could get anywhere by using slower, less convenient roads, but I always worried that he would take the easier, and more dangerous, option. One night he borrowed my car as usual and promised that he would, also as usual, avoid the treacherous road. During the evening I got an awareness that he had used that road. I was in bits while he was out. I sat in the lounge with the lights off, just waiting for the phone to ring, wondering if there would be bad news.

When I heard the car draw up and he walked in, as quietly as he could, the relief was enormous. I didn't say anything to him because I was in such an emotional state; in fact, he didn't even know I had been waiting. I went to bed and slept soundly, but the next morning I was absolutely furious because I knew, without a shadow of a doubt, that he had broken his promise and driven on that road. I marched into his room and gave him hell for it. Lying there, half asleep, with a ranting mother giving him a row for something she had psychically 'seen', he admitted it all.

'Is there anything you don't know?' he asked me, wearily.

'No! Nothing at all!' I said. But I was lying. There is plenty I don't know when it comes to my own family, and that's hard. Just like any other parent, I want to know that they're all always fine, that they're safe, that they're well, but I don't have that luxury as I can only see part of the picture. Maybe the children of psychics have more problems to contend with than most teenagers, but it was difficult for me as well.

I get snippets of information, but that's all. When I was pregnant myself, I didn't pick up anything about the babies. My neighbour was pregnant at the same time and when she told me she was having twins my response was one of horror. 'I'd die if that was me,' I thought. But just afterwards I had a scan and I remember looking at the screen and wondering how on earth the baby had moved from one side to the other and why there was still a shadow of it where I had seen it to begin with. It was only when the sonographer explained that I was having twins myself that the penny dropped, and of course I was delighted once I'd got used to the idea.

When my sister was pregnant, I told her not to bother with a scan as she was having twins. She said that was nonsense. As a midwife, she'd know. But I was right with her too. It was only with my own pregnancies that I saw absolutely nothing.

I have never had a sense of the babies who were coming. When I do readings for pregnant women, most of the time I'll be able to read the child's personality or character. With my own, I was in the dark. However, at the time I wasn't as aware of my talents as I am now. I was also very busy with life. As my own children grew up my gift started to get stronger, so perhaps if I'd had my children later in life I'd have picked up more signs.

Pregnancy and motherhood tend to make women reflect on the relationship they have, or have had, with their own mothers, and that was certainly the case for me. The child you were is growing into a mother who will nurture and care, and that in itself is a stage of your personal journey. When I was pregnant I would often imagine the type of parent I wanted to be, and I vowed that I would shower my children with love and warmth. I would never be distant or unsupportive, as my own parents had been with me. It brought back the way I had felt so alone and out of place in my early years, never knowing what to make of the things I saw and heard and sensed. When my mother died, I was twenty-four and a mum to four young children. A stage of my life had passed and it was time to come into myself. That is when I went back and looked at who I needed to become and how I should develop. Pregnancy is a time of reflection for all women, and I was no different in that sense, but it was motherhood and the death of my own mother that really developed my gifts.

I have always known whenever my children were upset by something they weren't telling me about, or have done something that they shouldn't have. Reading this, a lot of you will say, 'But most mums feel that way – it's mother's intuition.' If those are the words in your mind, great! I hope they are, because that is exactly what I'm trying to get over. We *all* have this ability, we *all* have the potential to harness this natural talent.

How many times have you been in a different room from your toddler and *just known* when you need to go through and check on them? And how many times has that been the very moment when they have stuck a bit of Lego in their mouth or decided to poke their fingers in the DVD player or make a move on the dog sleeping in the corner? Do you really think that's coincidence? I don't, and I know I'm not the only woman in the world to have this intuition. We all have it, but we aren't aware of the number of times it works. We just think we have some unidentified, unnamed 'link' with our children.

Even cynics will have experienced this, I'm sure. Why not take a moment to recall all the instances you can't quite explain? The times when you didn't want someone left alone with your child even though there was no clear reason not to. The times when you didn't want them to go on a trip but didn't know why. There *was* a reason; you were being sent a message, you were being given signs. At those moments you are in touch with your intuitive side, even if you are not normally that 'sort' of person. Female intuition, in particular, is very strong and it gets stronger when you have a child (unless there is no bonding, which happens in some sad cases). That is the very core of intuition or psychic awareness. Tuning in to your child's inner needs is incredibly basic and incredibly precious. It should not be under-rated and should always be acted upon. The more we act on our intuition, the better it will be for our children.

A funny feeling

How many times have you heard someone say they wished they had acted on 'a feeling'? How many times have you heard someone say that if they hadn't gone in to see their child at that moment, they would have fallen or choked or walked out into the road? All of these are indicators of how much help we can receive on our journey through life if only we listen and act upon the talents we are naturally blessed with. As mothers we have that ability – and as children we have it in an even purer form.

I remember doing a reading for a woman called Liz, who talked a lot about whether she 'believed' in things 'like this'. (I always find it funny when I hear this; if folk really didn't 'believe' then I can't see why they would ever contact me in the first place!) Such individuals often don't seem to see the relevance or importance of what they are telling me, and that was the case with Liz. She was the mother of three children, and grandmother to eight.

'What a week I've had,' she told me. 'My youngest grandson, who's only three months, was taken to hospital last night. My daughter was going to bed and just before she closed her eyes she felt she had to go and check on him. He'd been fed and he wasn't crying, but she had this feeling that she needed to look in on him. The poor wee thing had stopped breathing, and if she hadn't gone in that moment who knows what would have happened?'

'Why was he taken to hospital?' I asked.

'Well,' said Liz, 'just to see if there's anything wrong.'

I could have told her that her mother's intuition saved that child's life.

'That happened to me once as well,' Liz continued, 'with the same daughter I'm telling you about.'

'Is that right?' I said. 'Did anything else like that ever happen with your kids?'

'What do you mean?'

'Did you ever get a sense that there was something wrong, and go just in time to prevent something happening?'

'Oh yes,' said Liz. 'All the time. All mothers get that – don't they?'

Yes, I think they do. However, not all of them act on that intuition and most of them are completely oblivious to the fact that it is simply another one of their senses. Liz and her daughter were in tune with this aspect of their beings, but they had not yet recognised how to make the most of it. So far, they had reaped the benefits without looking too deeply into what was really happening, but the fact that Liz had experienced it so many times when her children needed her was proof enough for me. I had no doubt that if she and her daughter worked on developing their talents even more, and listening to their inner voices, their lives would be richer.

Very few people dispute that parent–child bonds exist, so why should there be resistance to taking this a step further and considering whether those bonds might be psychic ones? I think most people are unaware of how psychic they really are, but at one time or another they have had a 'funny feeling' that they've known something without ever having been told it. They know it but they don't know how they know it. If that isn't a psychic experience, then what is?

We don't just receive information through taste, touch, sight, smell and sound, but also through intuition and body language, through telepathy and primal instinct. Some talk about the sixth sense, which includes all of that second group, but we probably have many more than even six. 'Just knowing', 'gut instinct', 'just a feeling'

– we've all used these phrases, even the most cynical amongst us, and we should all act on the feelings they relate to. If we try and push our psychic abilities, they tend not to work – as you'll know if you have ever tried to *squeeze* those lottery numbers out. This is because we are thinking too hard rather than letting our psychic energy flow. We need to sense rather than think, daydream rather than focus.

Within all of this psychic wonder, the bonds between mother and child are incredible, like a psychic version of the umbilical cord. While the umbilical cord nourishes and grows the child physically, the psychic cord nourishes and grows the child in a different way. We send love and caring, protection and feelings to our children through this link, and it exists forever.

We all exchange psychic energy with each other all of the time, but in a mother's transactions with her child trust and protection are entrenched in their love for all of their journey through life. No matter what stage you are at in the process, remember that those in spirit are waiting to help us. We just need to open ourselves up to communicating with them and our children can show us the way. For those who are not parents, just spending time with children will help you to learn. By trusting our intuition around children, we can all have a more spiritual, more fulfilling journey through life.

Chapter 3

Lost and found

Sadly, not all pregnancies have happy outcomes. There have been occasions when I've predicted, or seen, the loss of babies who never reached the Earthly plane, and this presents problems for me when doing a reading. Should I refer to it or not? Is the person for whom I am reading ready to deal with it in a healthy way?

It is my personal view that, as souls, we've already made certain decisions about the life we will come here to live. We might choose to be on this plane for ninety years, just a few years, or we might even pass through without being born. What is important is that we complete whatever lesson it is necessary for us to learn, or teach. The ultimate goal is to expand the growth of the soul. Each time we come here with a different set of goals to add to the ones we have previously learned – or in some cases not learned, because there are people who continue to make the same mistakes over and over again. Mothers are a very special part of the wonderful journeys all souls make; in fact, those journeys would not be possible without them. I also believe that mothers make choices at some point about their own journeys, without being aware of it.

I realise that some readers will find this concept very hard to accept. They will never be able to imagine in some way having 'agreed' to the emotional pain and trauma of losing a child, for example. I speak from a higher spiritual perspective where there are concepts that are not always clear to those on this plane. When I went through my own darkness, before I understood these concepts, I would have considered such views to be nonsense but now I feel that there is a reason for everything. For all the pieces of the jigsaw to fall into place, everything in life must happen in a specific way.

It is necessary for us to complete each part of the journey by doing whatever we need to learn or teach. Any spirit can do one or the other, or a combination of both. I believe that women are hosts, in the nicest possible way, when they carry and give birth. You host a child into this world and prepare for the next stage when a soul will arrive and have an experience. Although we are responsible for our children until adulthood, it is up to them how they behave. As a mother, I find it hard to leave mine alone. I'm like a sheepdog herding them through life. But we all need to recognise that our children are here for their own journeys and we shouldn't really interrupt that. If they do something wrong, it is part of their learning and parents need to stand back as much as they can.

This is a difficult area to understand. If your child has made some bad choices, what should you do? For example, if they are taking drugs your instinct as a parent will, of course, be to intervene. However, I think there comes a point, especially if the child is close to adulthood, when you have little option. No matter what you do, they'll make their own choices. It is tough, but once you have looked after and protected them as a child you need to accept there is a cut-off point. You might not like that, you might not want it, but everyone makes their own choices and everyone has to go through their own learning process.

I'd like to emphasise that this is only my view, and I'm only one person. I don't have the answer to everything, nor have I walked a mile in someone else's shoes – but, if you are open to the idea of every soul being on a journey of experience, it may be useful to consider whether intervention by others is always the best approach.

Sarah's baby

My understanding of how the 'bigger picture' works is best shown through some amazing experiences I have had. On one occasion I was in a house in Liverpool doing readings for five women. After the first two, a young woman of about twenty-five, called Sarah, came in. Everything was straightforward to begin with. I told her about the work she would do and what she wanted from her life, and it was all perfectly accurate. Suddenly, from spirit, a child's energy appeared. I had to stop for a moment to gain a sense of what was happening and I realised that Sarah had lost a baby. I raised this with her and she revealed to me that she had indeed miscarried very recently. No one else knew about it. In fact, no one else had even known that Sarah was pregnant.

I could tell that she was scared about something, even though the pregnancy was over, and she confided that she was due to go into hospital the next day for a procedure to make sure that every part of the foetus and placenta was removed. This poor girl had such a mix of emotions surrounding her. She was grieving for her lost child, holding everything in as she hadn't even gone public about the pregnancy before it ended, and terrified of the operation. However, she also had a sense of anger and guilt about her. I soon saw that she blamed herself for what had happened. Now, this is an area I feel very strongly about. While there are, of course, actions women can take that can damage their unborn children, I also believe that there are some souls who were never meant to be born. I'm not talking about babies who are lost through their mothers' abuse of drink or drugs, or those who die because of some terrible accident, but of those who are simply not for this world.

Many will find this hard to understand, or may not want to understand, but it links into what I said earlier about us all choosing who our parents will be, even when that choice will bring difficult life experiences. It is all part of the journey we must take to make us stronger and better. Some souls agree to a contract whereby they will never be part of the Earthly plane, but their presence in the womb, even if it is only for a short while, will develop them or the woman who carries them for those few weeks or months. I know this explanation may be upsetting for anyone who has experienced unimaginable loss or tragedy, but it is simply my own belief, one that has evolved throughout my years on this plane as a psychic and also throughout my previous lives. We all have a journey to take, and we can't expect to see the bigger picture while we are so intimately involved in one single part of that journey.

I knew, without doubt, that Sarah had not caused this miscarriage but I could also understand the pain and anger she felt at herself. It is the woman who carries the child, and when that child is lost before it has reached full term, blaming herself is the natural thing for a mother to do. Sarah was full of remorse. I tried to explain to her my belief that an energy or spirit only comes here for as long as it needs to – in some cases only for minutes, in some for a week, in some for ninety years. Sarah's baby had been here for as long as it needed.

The more she carried the guilt with her, the longer the negative impact would remain. She wanted a baby, but if she kept thinking that way she would be weighed down by heavy, negative, sorrowful energy. That doesn't create a happy, inviting environment for another baby. I wasn't underestimating Sarah's grief – and would never underestimate any woman's grief, as I've been there myself – but you can't change what's happened. You can only change how you look at things and your attitude towards the past to allow you to move on in the best possible way.

Some women miscarry very early on in a pregnancy, but they still need to know that wee soul is all right. When I give them that confirmation, I can almost see their worry lift. I meet many women who have never told anyone about their lost babies, but I can see them all. Once I tell them that, they know that the life they once held inside them, for a brief moment, mattered. It is still their child, their little one, and they still have maternal feelings towards it, so once they know that the soul is happy and forgiving it can change their whole energy. I have done readings for women in their seventies and eighties who have lost babies fifty or more years earlier, but they still think of them, and they still take comfort when I give them that recognition.

The responsibility that comes with this gift I have been blessed with is something I never take for granted or treat in a blasé manner. I often have to be a counsellor as much as a psychic. I explained to Sarah why some pregnancies end early and told her my sense that she would definitely have another child in the very near future – which she did. I told her that the baby she had lost would be with her in spirit as she went through her next pregnancy and would give her tremendous support.

Losing babies

Realising that a baby isn't meant to be is a terribly sad thing and I feel for any woman who goes through it. Soon after I'd had my four children, I discovered that I was pregnant again. My immediate thought was, 'I can't cope.' I already had four children under five years of age and simply didn't know how I would manage. The thought that I might be carrying twins again made the fear even greater. I couldn't stop thinking about the fact that I didn't want to be pregnant and I even considered ending the pregnancy, which was against every nurturing bone in my body. When I miscarried, I was distraught because I knew, in my heart of hearts, that I would have loved that baby just as much as I did the others. I would have coped somehow, no matter how bleak the picture seemed. The day I started bleeding, I knew it was over, and I blamed myself completely. I was convinced that my negative way of thinking had brought on the miscarriage.

Sometimes, when I do a reading for a woman, I can tell she's had a termination. There's no way of confusing it with a miscarriage. First of all, I have the sense of a sudden ending; and secondly, in all honesty, that's often why the woman has come to me in the first place. With a miscarriage there is more of a gentle progression to spirit. I've often heard women say that they have carried guilt about terminations for years, but I don't believe any of us has a right to judge. Whatever a woman goes through is part of her journey on this plane.

Recently, I read for a woman who I knew had a child in spirit. 'I can see a small white coffin,' I told her, and it was obvious that this was a child who had been stillborn rather than miscarried or terminated. Her eyes filled up straight away. The rawness of the emotions where babies are concerned is never far from the surface, and I held her hand as I said that I could also see a little white teddy bear at the side and several other little trinkets in the coffin. She was filled with joy at the thought that her baby, wherever she was, still had the trinkets that she had lovingly placed in the coffin for her. A teddy bear, a rose and a photograph were all very clear to me. It is comforting for people to know that type of thing – and it's uplifting too. The spirit of the baby wants the mum to know that it has these mementoes and that it appreciates the fact that she put them there.

I advise every woman who loses a baby to be gentle with herself, and to create a positive emotional environment for any other babies who may be waiting. It could be easier said than done, but it's what those in spirit would want. You have to grieve but you have to think to the future as well by making the best energy you possibly can. I advise women to imagine a golden light in their womb, which makes it an energetic place ready for the new soul to come into.

Reading for Olivia

I knew a woman called Olivia whose baby had died only months after it was born with severe cerebral palsy. Olivia kept asking me for a reading but I didn't think that she was in the correct frame of mind to have one, so I put her off. When people are still in deep mourning they can misinterpret readings and take negative implications from them that aren't there, so I will try to make them wait till their outlook is more positive. One day, Olivia rang and asked for a reading again, and this time the energy around her felt different, so I agreed. I began the session with information about her work. She was being manipulated by a woman who was fearful for her own position, and this was making for a very toxic working environment. I told Olivia that she should detach herself from this negative relationship. The matter would be resolved whether or not she did anything, but it would be for the best if she distanced herself from it.

I was trying to keep the reading away from Olivia's baby as I was still unsure whether she was in the right place to discuss it. I also felt very strongly that what she was going through at work was draining her so much that I hoped I could steer her in a direction that would help. However, I began to get a sense of her baby coming through. If it were not for the fact that I trust spirit implicitly, I would not have carried on with the reading. I had to listen to and recognise what I was being sent. It was quite clear that the child – a little girl – had moved on in spirit and was being well cared for by her grandmother, Olivia's mother, who had passed with cancer in her early fifties. The child told me that Olivia needed to know many things: not just that her mother was caring for her, but that she had always known her time on the Earth plane was to be limited. She wanted Olivia to know that she was grateful to her for allowing this to happen, as it was necessary for her spiritual progression.

I relayed this information with great care, as the most important thing to me is the emotional well-being of the person I am reading for. This is top of my agenda at all times and I was concerned that Olivia might be angry that I was passing on a message which could have been seen as insensitive.

'I want you to know that I am giving you these words from your child,' I told her. 'She sends them with love and she is indebted to you for allowing yourself to be part of her journey. She knows it was hard and she knows that it still hurts, but, without you, she would not have known such love and she would not be able to move on.'

To my surprise, and absolute relief, Olivia understood immediately. This showed what a remarkable woman she was and totally backed up what her daughter had said about her. Olivia smiled and said that it made much more sense now. She said that she had been reading lots of books about how and why spirits come to the Earth plane, and she realised that sometimes it wasn't for long. Olivia said that if I had told her these things when she had asked for a reading before, she would not have been equipped to deal with it, but now, although she was still grieving, she appreciated what had happened. The fact that her daughter was with her meant a lot and the fact that they had both learned from each other would stay with her forever.

This was such a touching story that it has stayed with me as well. Olivia was a gracious and brave lady, and I feel that her child was spot on when she said it took a remarkable individual to allow the next stage of her journey to occur.

Moving on

Women who miscarry often conceive again quite quickly, and that can be a blessing. Sometimes it is a gift from the little one who has passed. If a new pregnancy doesn't happen as quickly as you may wish, you should look on it as your healing time. However, if you can't move on emotionally you may be preventing your child from moving on too. Whether it is in practical terms, such as keeping a nursery exactly the same when there is no baby to put in it, or if you keep bursting into tears the whole time, be aware that your child is watching you. They are with you in spirit, and they can't feel free to do what they need to do while you are still laden down with grief and negativity.

When a baby – or a child – passes, the most loving thing a mother can do is grieve, accept that it has moved to spirit, let go and put it in a place where the experience can be healthy. Of course it is an awful thing to go through, but living in a shrine to a lost loved one, or spending every minute of every waking hour thinking of them, helps no one – including the soul who has passed over.

Here are some ideas of ways in which you can move through your grief by making a connection with your child in spirit.

- Writing a letter to spirit is a lovely thing to do – you can keep it, burn it, let it drift away, it doesn't matter. It's the intention that counts.

- Take some quiet time to think of all you loved about your child and the happiness you feel when you think of them – focus on the positive. I'm not suggesting that there isn't hurt, but it will help you so much to take a moment to think only of the good things. If the pain is very new or very raw, you may only be able to do this for two minutes, one minute, even thirty seconds at a time. That's fine. Do what you can, and you can build on it. If you lost a baby through miscarriage, think of the joy you felt when you got your first positive test – your baby will feel that joy. If you went through the agony of stillbirth, think of those times when your baby kicked inside you – your baby will feel that joy too. Your pain is real, but you did have happy moments; don't lose them, because they were real too.

- Send out love and thanks to your child, and tell them that you give them the freedom to move on in spirit. This will help you, because by them moving on they will be able to make their presence felt to you much more often and much more explicitly.

- Recognise that they are with you and look out for signs of this – a feather where one shouldn't really be, things moved when you know you put them somewhere quite specific, a breeze on a still day, a rainbow when there has been no rain. Those in spirit love to communicate with us and get terribly frustrated when we don't see what they are doing – help them!

We're all here to live, we're all here to experience, and if we don't do that we can't move on. I knew of one woman who had two children with her and two in spirit. Whenever she met anyone new she would say that she was a mother of four – which she was. However, this prompted the other person to ask questions and she would then have to explain that two had passed. Every new relationship she formed began with her bringing up her grief and becoming upset. Now I fully accept that she is a mother of four, but there is something to be said for not allowing that way of thinking to define you. It becomes a habit, like carrying a sack of coal on your shoulders that gets heavier and heavier with each day. It becomes a learned behaviour – but learned behaviours can be broken.

When a woman comes to me who has a child in spirit, I will always count that child amongst the ones she 'has', because that is appropriate in the context of a reading. If I say, 'You've got three children,' and she replies, 'No, I had three, but one died. I have two now,' I will refute that as I can see three when I look at her; she has three in her universal family. It's about recognising the right things at the right times in a way that allows you to make the most of your time on this plane and to progress in your life's journey. A mother who is constantly upset about a baby she has lost doesn't love that child any more than a mother who can see the beauty and happiness in life. Love can't be measured that way.

I once met a woman called Harriet, who came to me for a general reading. She was a lovely lady, but it quickly became clear that she had a child's energy around her, which was affecting every part of her life. I could see that the baby had been a stillbirth. I did what I always did and provided Harriet with information that I couldn't possibly have known unless it was being passed to me, and then I had to move on to the very difficult subject of her baby. The reason it was so difficult to broach was because Harriet was still badly affected by the loss of her child. The little one had passed almost ten years earlier, but Harriet carried the grief in her mind and her heart every single day. The baby who had passed wanted her mother to move on — not to forget, but to get to a stage in her life when she was allowing happiness and welcoming the future, rather than always being bogged down in the past. I knew that Harriet herself would find this a very hard message to receive — in fact, I wasn't sure she would welcome it at all.

In the event, when I described her beautiful daughter in spirit and provided her with evidence of what I knew to be true, she was more open to the words her daughter passed through me than I had anticipated. Maybe it was time for the past to be put to rest. Sometimes people come for a reading at exactly the right moment in their lives. Often they will begin our chat by saying, 'I don't really know why I'm here,' or 'I've never done this sort of thing before but I just felt I had to come and see you.' They don't seem to realise that the spirits facilitated their visit for a reading. The signs and messages may have been there for some time, but a moment arrives when all is aligned and suddenly even someone who has previously been terribly closed will open up to the wonder which exists all around us.

This was the case with Harriet. She didn't make rash promises – I'm not sure I would have believed her had she done so – and she didn't commit to changing over-night, but she left with some of the weight lifted from her shoulders. I reassured her that her daughter was happy, and that she had a right to be happy too. In some ways, it was hard for her to accept that her child was happy as she still felt the loss so keenly, but she took the first steps on her journey to recovery that night.

There will be many women reading this who have lost babies before it was their time for this world, and these words may bring up old memories for them, but I hope they have found comfort over the years. It doesn't matter what age a woman is; she never forgets the ones she has lost. I imagine many men feel the same way, but most people who come to me for readings are women, so that's the area I know best. What I would like those parents to do is take a moment to send their love to the babies they have lost. If you have never allowed them to go, to grow in spirit, try to find the strength for that to happen now. As they grow, you will grow too. As you send them love, you will receive love. In no way will this mean that you have forgotten – that will never happen – but you are acknowledging and honouring them. You are giving respect by saying how lovely it was that they were here at all. Of course, you are sorry that they had to pass, but you can still hope that they are growing in spirit and that you will make a commitment to grow too.

There will still be a connection; there always will be. You can still love your child. Speak to them as much as you ever did, if that's what comforts you, but do it with a lighter heart. Tell them what you intend to do that day, point out the flowers and the sunshine when you go for a walk, and understand that your child wants to see you happy.

If this chapter has triggered anything for you, then please take it in a positive way. Follow the practical advice on page 52. Write a letter to your baby. Light a candle to them. Go to the beach and shout to them as the waves crash. Then move on. You can go back whenever you want – nothing is closed off – but try to see the wonder in this life too. I can assure you that's what your baby in spirit will want.

Lucy's brother

Children who pass over often become the spirit guide for someone in their family. I've come across this time and time again. On one occasion I was doing a reading for a woman in her mid-forties called Lucy. Like most people who come for readings she wanted to know about work and romance, and everything was coming through pretty easily. Then I stopped because I got a very clear sense that she was more in tune with the spirit world than she was letting on.

'Do you ever feel the presence of a spirit with you?' I asked, knowing full well that she did. When she admitted it, I felt free to tell her more. 'There's a wee boy in the spirit world who gets your attention more than most, isn't there?'

Lucy agreed again.

'To me, it feels like your brother. Is it? Have you lost a brother at some point in your life?'

She told me her big brother had died of leukaemia when she was only a toddler.

'He's there to be with you,' I told her. 'He is there to assist you in your life and help keep you on the right path. Do you know what I mean?'

'Kind of,' Lucy answered, 'but I don't really know how I can work out what I'm meant to do. Is he sending me messages?'

I tried to explain. 'You're very psychic but you're scared at the same time. There's a part of you that wants to take your gift forward but you're not sure how to do this. I sense that there's also a part of you that doesn't know if it's right. Am I correct?'

Lucy nodded. I notice this in a lot of people; even if they are intuitive they still have some residual wariness about how appropriate their feelings and senses are. In my opinion there is nothing *more* appropriate, but not everyone has that secure knowledge.

'Your brother is here to ensure that you follow your path. Be guided by him. He wouldn't lead you into danger or allow you to be drawn to anything that wasn't good for you. He may not be on this plane, but he still has your best interests at heart – he's still your big brother. He will be your guide for the time being and this may or may not change depending on how your development progresses. Be open to what you feel, act on your intuition, and you will blossom – he'll make sure of that.'

Lucy said that she felt such relief that I had brought all of this up and confirmed what she had always felt – that her brother was there beside her. She said that she had barely known him, but actually that wasn't strictly true. He had been beside her all of her life in one form or another, and, as we chatted further, she told me many examples of times when he had clearly been communicating with her. A brother's love, or a sister's love, does not fade or disappear because they have passed over, and Lucy was a remarkable woman in that she had an awareness of her spiritual connection. I only hoped that she would take what I had given her and use it to move forward in the rest of her life; thankfully, her next words made me feel that this had a real chance of happening.

'I want to take this as far as I can,' she told me. 'I want to make a real start on developing myself.'

I told her that she could go to a spiritualist church and also recommended some books to set her on her way, but emphasised that the most important thing was that she should listen to her brother and follow her intuition. That was the biggest gift that she could give both of them.

Lucy has kept in touch with me since then and her journey has been an inspirational one, as has that of her brother. I know that her mother and father, not the sort of people who would have believed in 'this sort of thing', have actually become very open-minded as they have witnessed concrete examples of their daughter's talent. Lucy has been able to pass on information about the son they lost, and they have realised that she is indeed communicating with her brother. In doing so, she has brought all of the family together again, and given her parents tremendous peace.

The face in the window

Those who have not lost a child can never fully understand the pain and emptiness of those who have. We can sympathise but never empathise. It would be terrible of me to say that there is nothing to grieve as your child is still here, albeit on a different plane, because that would underestimate the horrific emotional cost of a child's death. However, I would gently suggest that there are ways to channel your grief and perhaps to look at whether signs remain of your son's or daughter's continuing involvement in your life.

The idea of reincarnation can be very helpful to people who have lost children. For some it may be an unthinkable notion, a step too far – but why? If you have ever thought to yourself that a child has 'been here before' or that they are 'old beyond their years' then surely the logical progression is to consider reincarnation?

It is difficult to find healing energy after loss. For a time you will feel despair and you may feel as if you will never be happy again. You won't want anyone to tell you that you need to move on or that time will heal, but it's true. In my experience, the child who has passed may also need some help.

One woman, Diane, asked me to come and do a reading as their son kept seeing a face at their window. Diane told me that her little boy, Nathan, was very disturbed by it and that no one else could see what he was seeing. She told me that there was no way anyone was playing a prank, and that the face Nathan could see was that of a baby.

I went along to their house one night. First of all I noted that there was definitely no way anyone could get access to the first-floor windows from outside. I started doing a reading for Diane while Nathan, who was about six, played on the floor with his toy cars. I asked him how he was, what school he went to, and lots of little questions like that. He answered them in a friendly fashion, then asked me why I was there.

'I'm here to see this baby your mum has told me about,' I informed him.

Immediately, he seemed terror-stricken. 'No! No! You shouldn't look at it!' he cried. 'It's too scary!' The wee soul was absolutely distraught.

Very calmly, I said, 'All right – that's fine,' but he wouldn't calm down.

'It just appears at the window,' he continued. 'I'll be here playing, and it just appears! It just appears!'

'That's fine, Nathan,' I said quietly, 'but here's a thing. Have you ever asked it *why* it appears?'

He looked at me as if thinking, *'She's mad. Why would I talk to a baby's face at my window?'*

'It's what I would do,' I told him. 'I'd ask the baby why it was here and what it wanted.'

I was trying to make light of it and not pass on any of the terror that I suspected his mum had displayed, but I also wanted to put the suggestion in his mind that if you ask questions, sometimes you get answers. Diane was sitting beside me, and I suspect she thought I was off my trolley. I could almost hear her thinking, *'This thing appears at the window and you want us to have a cosy wee chat asking why it's popped in for the night?'*

I continued with Diane's reading and wasn't too surprised when I discovered that she had miscarried a baby the year before Nathan was born. I broached the subject gently.

'Diane, I'm getting the sense that you've suffered a loss as a mother. Is that right?' She confirmed it but I knew that I had to tread cautiously if I was to link that child with the baby who had been appearing to her son.

'Sometimes,' I told her, 'the spirit of a child needs to come back. They may have a message to pass on, or they may just be checking up on those who are still here. They don't mean us to be scared, but if we don't know what's going on sometimes that is exactly what happens.'

'Oh my God,' Diane exclaimed. 'Is that what's happening? Is the baby at the window my baby?'

'I think so,' I told her.

After I had done the reading, I left them. I didn't mention the baby again and I didn't give them any 'instructions'. I thought it best just to leave them to turn things over in their own minds. Diane called me a few days later. She and Nathan had been sitting in the lounge when he said that the face was at the window again. Before Diane could respond, Nathan shouted out, 'What do you want?'

She told me it was as if there was a feeling of relief in the room, and then Nathan turned to his mum, smiling, and said, 'It just wants to play!'

Sometimes, spirits simply want a bit of recognition. Once you acknowledge them, things can change completely. Diane and Nathan never saw that baby again.

Parents are very good at transferring their fears, and children like Nathan respond accordingly. The fact that they were both more relaxed, and that Nathan took the step of asking the question, allowed Diane's baby to feel recognised and to move on. Initially, it appeared to be a very scary thing, but once it was put back into proportion it was easier to deal with.

Sometimes it is pure imagination. I've gone into places where spirits have reportedly been seen and had to say, 'Actually, there's nothing here.' But sometimes there is spirit, and that spirit wants something very simple, such as a few words or a warm thought.

Please don't dive off the deep end if you have a similar experience. It may help to know that the spirit of your child is still there and that, if you don't move on, neither will your child. Whether your loss has been through miscarriage or stillbirth, through the passing of a baby, toddler, teenager or grown-up child, time will have changed for you, and it will be divided into 'before' and 'after'. I believe that, once contact has been made, that can change too. It can be turned into 'before you understood' and 'after you came to awareness'. Your child won't come back in life form to this plane, and your arms may still feel empty, but you don't have to be alone.

On this plane we lose many loved ones – but we can find so many of them too, if we only know how to open our eyes, hearts and minds. I hope this is something you all find the strength to do because what you will receive in return is immeasurable.

Chapter 4

Learning and loving

None of us knows everything. If we did, we wouldn't be here. We all need to learn and we all need to accept that we need to learn. Some of us are better at it than others, and some of us are lucky enough to have tremendous help from those who have loved us and continue to love us on the other side. If we need their help, we only have to ask for it. I hope that I can teach you all to speak that language from the heart.

Children are often our guides, because their innocence coexists with great intelligence. They have the ability to see many things that adults cannot. Their emotional and spiritual intelligence allows them to be remarkably psychic as well as skilled at passing messages from the other side. I feel blessed that I have been given the privilege of being able to work with both sides. I shelved my own gift around the age of eleven, trying to steer away from it because no on was encouraging me, but I reconnected with it later in life and am grateful for all the opportunities this has given me. It was a learning curve I needed to travel. Learning can be hard. We don't always want to hear what we need to do to move forwards, and sometimes it can be my role to pass on difficult messages. In this chapter I will explain some ways in which lessons can be learned – in this life and beyond.

Children with addictions

Those of us who are mothers are 'hardwired' to feel enormous love for our children, no matter what they do. I have had many people contact me with heartbreaking stories of children who have gone off the rails, perhaps because of addictions and bad choices. When the parent's grief becomes too much to bear, they are often sent to me by the spirits for advice. I've seen lots of distraught mothers whose efforts to save their children are making absolutely no difference whatsoever, and to them I say that when you reach a point when you don't feel you can do anything else, when you feel helpless, simply send them all your love and a sense of peace. Sometimes they will pick this up and sometimes not. You can't influence their choices but you can continue to act in a loving and parental way, by sending beautiful energy.

I've done several readings for mothers whose children have gone to spirit after years of drug abuse, and in this instance I am able to tell them that their children change when they go to spirit. They don't have the physical body or the obsessive need they had on this plane. They have pure love now, and drink, drugs and other addictions don't even register.

However, when I act as the conduit for their messages, the addict who has passed comes through to me the same way as they were in life. They will be stoned or high or drunk, and it's quite a horrible feeling to pick up because it makes me feel the same way. Sometimes I don't even know what's going on. I can't speak properly; it takes over, and the person I'm with usually recognises it immediately.

When someone contacts me who has lost a child through addiction, I try to reconnect them with the love they felt for that child. If a child passes because of their addiction, it can be easy to reflect only on the bad times, but I advise parents to recall the times when they loved their child, when they did so much for them, when they laughed together and were each other's worlds – because that time can and will come again.

Once the fuzziness of the intoxication passes, I get the child the way they were 'before', the true essence of the person they were. Generally, they want to tell their loved ones that they shouldn't blame themselves for the addiction. I can pass on messages to reassure both parties that the love is still there and that there are good memories too. The child who has passed is in a much better place and is usually keen to tell their mum – or other loved one – that they had no idea what was going on a lot of the time, that they were crazy, and that it is all in the past now.

People who have passed due to drug or drink addictions tend to feel a lot of remorse – not for themselves, but for what they have done to their family. The sadness of what could have been tends to linger. There are a lot of mixed-up feelings, and amongst them can be anger. Looking back, they usually can't believe that they did what they did, but they don't feel regret as such, because, as spirit, they know that it was part of their journey. Once a child is in spirit they will know and see all that their parents did for them, and they will recognise the commitment and sacrifice they made.

Caring from the other side

The bonds that exist between mother and child don't fade just because one party has moved on, but sometimes even I am taken aback by the strength of love, which exists and grows. A few years ago I was heading down to Hemel Hempstead to do a show. I arrived at the hotel and settled myself in, getting ready for the night ahead. When I am preparing for a show I always clear my mind as much as possible and tell the spirits that I am ready to take their messages for that evening. This gives them 'warning' and sometimes acts as a psychic kick up the backside for the ones who might usually be a bit shy.

The first spirit who came through to me in my room was a young girl, around the age of fourteen, who called herself Julie. She was a beautiful lass, with long brown hair, thick with curls, and she was very chatty and friendly. She started telling me what her life had been like, and that she had been thinking about studying to become a graphic designer once she left school. Julie kept talking about how she was good at design and liked to keep herself busy, and it was flowing very naturally. It can be sad to communicate with children whose lives have been cut short, but I always try to remember that they themselves don't feel this loss as they are happy where they are.

However, Julie's mood changed when she began to talk about her mum. *'Mum's not been well,'* she told me. *'She's been going to hospital and they think it's a bronchial problem. Now they want her to be admitted so that they can run some tests.'*

I asked Julie what was bothering her and she gave me the kind of reply that I hear from many who have passed.

'Mum takes care of everyone and I want to take care of her – but there's only so much I can do,' she said. *'I just want to make sure she's all right; she's the one who needs to be taken care of now.'*

I told Julie that I would do all I could to speak with her mum if she came to the show that night, but she was still unsettled.

'There's something else,' she said. 'Our next-door neighbour has lost her little dog. They've put out flyers to see if anyone knows where it is, but no one has called. She loves that dog and she's so worried in case it's dead.'

Julie was getting quite upset, and I worry when that happens to someone in spirit because they generally have a very balanced persona once they are removed from the pettiness of what goes on in our plane.

I waited to hear what she would say next, as sometimes it is important just to listen rather than ask lots of questions.

'I had cancer,' she whispered. 'Everyone was so good to me. It was bad and I was in such pain but my mum never stopped looking after me for a second. Our neighbours all helped, everyone cared so much. Then one day it all stopped. Everything stopped and I wasn't there any more. I'm not there now when they all need me. I wish I could help, I wish I could give something back.'

I really hoped that I would be able to pass on Julie's message at the show that night. I had no doubt that her mum would be there, because that is why Julie came through to me in the first place. She knew. As soon as the show started, Julie came back. Although she had passed her messages to me earlier, it wasn't unusual for her to return. Spirits tend to like to be present when the connection is made with their loved one. It's also better for me as it helps to keep the link strong.

I told the audience that I had a young girl of about fourteen by the name of Julie, who had been taken by cancer. I gave a few geographical and medical details before seeing one woman raise her hand tentatively and I knew it was Julie's mum. I told her that Julie was worried that she had a bronchial problem, and at that she sat up and took notice. I backed it up with the knowledge that she was going into hospital for a few days for tests, and also that Julie knew about the neighbour's dog going missing. This was proof that I had a real link with her daughter. I even gave details from the 'lost dog' posters that Julie was showing me.

I said that I could tell Julie was a beautiful, upbeat girl who loved to chat when she was here on the Earth plane and that she was still the same on the other side. Julie's mum was upset, as most parents are when their child comes through, but this was in a good way. She had a sense of comfort that her daughter had not disappeared; her energy was still there. I felt that Julie's energy was much more settled and at peace once the connection had been made and she got the message across to her mum. I felt that her mum would be fine now. I had given her proof that helped her to see beyond the veil and learn a new way of looking at things. Both spirit and Earth plane were at ease as a result of the bridge I'd been able to build.

Past life connections

For me, it is always hard when children who have passed come through, even though I know that they are happy and settled on the other side. It's a heartbreaking situation for any parent, and I feel for them. At least in a small way, the messages I transmit bring comfort and provide a connection, a spiritual link that is invaluable for learning what has to be learned in order to progress. This can be a lesson from the present Earth plane or sometimes a person has to make a connection with a previous life they have lived in order to feel complete.

I should explain a bit more here about my belief in reincarnation. To my mind, this Earth plane isn't our last stop – it's just one of the stations along the way as we learn and develop. I am no authority on reincarnation, but I feel that when we pass over there is a kind of evaluation – not in a religious sense but the sense that we look at what we have achieved or learned while on the Earth plane. That's when we ask if we have done what we set out to do on our path. What did we learn from our visit? If you have done nothing, learned nothing, then there will be the option to come back in a reincarnated form to see if your destiny can be fulfilled, to see if you can learn and achieve.

However, even if you answer 'yes', if you have learned, if you have achieved, then there is still the option to come back and experience more. Many will come back and become a guide to someone on the Earth plane to assist their growth and, in so doing, help with their own.

If we pass over and are evolved enough to believe that there is a choice about returning to Earth, then this has to stay firmly fixed in the mind. This is what Buddhists do. If you have a fixed idea, I believe it will happen, but if you pass thinking that you do not have a choice, or you just don't know what to believe, then there is a strong possibility that you will keep returning as often as you need to in order to learn. Sometimes it is my role to help people understand this, and to know how they need to grow in order to progress.

I once went to do some readings for a family in Inverness. When I got to the house, the woman introduced herself and her daughter who was called Kathleen. She told me that two of her other daughters had planned to be there but that they couldn't make it – one of them had a car breakdown and the other had been called into work. People are apologetic about that sort of thing, but I tend to think it happens for a reason, because the spirits have decided it should be this way, and as I looked at Kathleen I suspected that *she* was the reason. I would be able to give her more focus without the other readings to do, which was what spirit must have wanted in the first place. I got an immediate feeling that this girl, who appeared to be in her late teens, had been here before.

I did a reading for the mum and then moved on to Kathleen. I use Tarot cards for readings because they allow me to tap into the person's life and see what is going on, then point them in particular directions. If spirit comes through, I will also pass on any messages they have. I asked Kathleen to shuffle the cards and then to select a few. Before I laid them out I took a chance by saying to her, 'I have a feeling you've been here before.'

'Me too!' she replied.

'I have the sense that you lived in America many years ago.'

Kathleen nearly fell off her chair at that. Her eyes widened and she became very emotional. 'I've been waiting for someone to say that for so long,' she admitted. 'I needed to know that it was true – I've always felt it so strongly.'

'You lived there without a doubt. I'm also getting that you were involved in politics, that your father was something to do with the Civil War. I bet you've always been drawn to that era, haven't you?'

She nodded in agreement again and told me that ever since she was a little girl she had always felt an affinity with everything to do with America around the time of the Civil War. When she'd studied it in high school she felt as if she knew everything already. I asked her if it felt like reading about home, and she lit up. 'That's exactly what it felt like,' she said.

I told her that a lot of things she was experiencing in this life were linked to what she had gone through in a previous existence. I felt that her American life had ended when she was a child. I had a feeling that she would be drawn to a job in which she was helping children. She agreed with this too and I pointed out that her calling would be a combination of wanting to give something back to society, wanting to raise awareness about prejudice and inequality and make a change to other people's lives, as this had been so central to her father's agenda when she was a child.

Kathleen said that she really wanted to go to America now, and I told her that it would happen, but there was no rush – she had plenty of lifetimes to achieve that goal.

This kind of experience reaffirms the cycle of life we all go through. If more of us understood the links between each part of our existence, we would be better placed to make good choices about what we commit ourselves to; that was certainly the case with Kathleen and she isn't the only person I've come across who has needed to make that correlation.

The call of Africa

The process of universal energy works in mysterious ways. I went to one woman's house to do readings for her and her daughter Rebecca. When I went in, I couldn't help looking at Rebecca because I couldn't work out what she was doing there. She needed to be in the Far East, from what I could tell. I could see the country Thailand. Now, I usually only read to people who are eighteen or over and she seemed quite young, but her mum confirmed her age; however, she also said it was unlikely Rebecca would get anything from me, as she had seen many psychics in the past and they had never been able to give her any information. I assured them both that this certainly wouldn't be the case this time as I could tell that Rebecca was full of universal energy and there was a message just waiting for her. They took turns to come in and see me on their own, and Rebecca was first.

'Before you take a card, or even shuffle them,' I said, 'I just need to ask if you believe in reincarnation.'

She broke into a wide smile. 'Absolutely!' she said, happily.

'Then you won't think I'm off my head!' I laughed. 'I'm drawn to Thailand with you. It's as if you're here physically, but you shouldn't be – you're meant to be there. You're drawn to that culture, aren't you? And I bet you have been ever since you were a child?'

Rebecca confirmed all of this and said that when she was a little girl she desperately sought out books about Thailand and used to have a notebook that detailed everything she knew about the place – the culture, religion, spices and fabrics. We spoke about it further and I was able to tell her about many things she had felt a link to during her life, then it became clear that we needed to talk about her career. Rebecca was currently working as a hairdresser and was finding it very unfulfilling. She told me that she was thinking about going to university to study law, but when she said it, again I got a very clear feeling that this wasn't for her either. Suddenly I got a distinct message that she needed to go to Africa, not Thailand after all. I passed this on.

'I don't believe it,' she said. 'I've been looking into doing voluntary work with children in Africa.'

This made sense to me. Linking into her spirit still further, I could explain what was happening. 'When you were in Thailand in a previous life,' I told her, 'you were someone who was regal – and you didn't give back. You need to return somewhere to do something you should have done last time.' Rebecca had always known that there was a purpose she needed to fulfil.

When her mum came into the room and Rebecca told her what had transpired, the older woman was incredulous because it fitted in with what she had observed in her daughter all of her life. 'I have a son as well,' she said, 'and he has always wanted to live elsewhere too.'

As soon as she said that, I knew that the boy needed to be in Hong Kong. This woman had no qualms at all about her children being drawn to places that they had been linked to in past lives. 'Isn't it lovely,' I said to her, 'that you were host to two children who have had these wonderful experiences?'

'That's exactly how I feel,' she replied. 'They came here but they obviously need to do different things in different parts of the world. From when they were small, this was clear.'

To me, she was tapping into the psychic consciousness and intuitive energy that all children experience, but which some parents cannot – or will not – support. If you can give your child that support you will be helping their journey, not just in this life, but throughout their whole existence on every plane.

Kasey's mum

The idea of reincarnation can be soothing when someone has passed, but there are times when the knowledge that another loved one is looking after a child in spirit can be a great comfort too. The most beautiful thing about spirits is that they can be our guides if we just listen to what is being said.

I did a reading for a woman called Kasey who had a difficult marriage. There was nothing that couldn't be sorted but she worried enormously about the fact that her relationship could easily be lost. I spent some time talking to her about her marriage, and then brought in her mother from spirit. She was a very strong lady whom Kasey missed very much. The mother told me, with great concern, all about her daughter on the Earth plane. She said that Kasey had had a miscarriage and that she and her husband were both in great pain, but were unable to talk to each other about it. I mentioned that Kasey seemed to be in a world of her own most of the time and it was hard for others to know what she was thinking, and her mum agreed with me. This could have been one factor affecting her marriage. It's hard to be close to a person who is emotionally closed.

When I mentioned the miscarriage to Kasey, she broke down, but they weren't tears of grief. She felt emotional comfort on hearing that the little one was being cared for because she had been terribly concerned for its safety. All of this information settled her and actually made her relationship with her husband better. She opened up emotionally to him and together they worked on what they had.

Spirit coming in to speak with her made a huge impact on Kasey's life. This is what makes everything worthwhile for me. I love it when I see a change in a person. It's as if the strain leaves their face and body and they relax completely. The spirit world can bring amazing gifts through their messages.

My role as intermediary

We can all learn a lot about love from those on the other side, and from the angels as well. Most people think of angels as light, shiny beings with wings, but there are other kinds. I believe that children can be angels as well, whether in spirit or on the Earthly plane. These children are the ones who can guide us, and all we need to do is take their hands.

Even though in my work I connect people on the Earthly plane to loved ones in spirit, I totally understand what it is like to need reassurance from spirit. When I lost my twins through miscarriage, my wee angels, I knew they were in spirit and fine. I felt them around me, but only from time to time. I went to see a medium to find out who would come through, and to my absolute delight I was given confirmation that they were with me. This sort of reading is always very emotional, but in a good way. It is a blessing to know that my angels were – and are – still there. This is what makes my work so important. I understand the pain people can be in when they come to me and help them to make a connection when they cannot themselves connect. This often allows them to move on in life, and I am honoured to be able to help.

Chapter 5

A lasting memory

It is my belief that, if we accept spirit, all of our ingrained assumptions and fears about loss and bereavement will become filtered through an entirely different lens. For example, as grown-up children ourselves we may find that parents who were lacking on the Earthly plane are doing a lot more for us on the other side.

I met Jacqueline at a show in Nottingham when I was contacted, almost immediately, by a man in spirit who said that he wanted me to pass on a message to his daughter in the audience. This man was full of fun and I could tell that he liked a drink; ironically enough, the phrase that came to mind was *'no angel'*. I asked if there was anyone who recognised the various little bits of information I gave out, such as geographical locations, and Jacqueline stood up. The man who was communicating with me said that she was indeed his daughter and told me her name.

When I passed on my impression of him, she said that it was spot on. I could tell that, although a bit of a character, he never meant any harm to anyone and had a big heart. Jacqueline was quite emotional as she confirmed everything I was saying. All of this was useful, but I knew that the man wanted me to pass on something else. Giving 'evidence' before I communicate the 'real' message is just the way I work. It gives a foundation to build on and subsequent messages can be grounded in trust.

I could see a small boy with this man in spirit and knew that the child was the centre of the message; he was the real – and only – reason that the man had made contact.

'Jacqueline,' I began, 'I'm talking with your dad and he has your child with him.'

'No, he doesn't,' she replied immediately. 'I don't have any kids.'

'Well,' I continued, 'he's telling me that you do and I can see them both together.'

'No,' she said, adamantly. 'You're wrong.'

I knew there was some delicate issue at stake but didn't know what. During a show, things are hectic. There are so many messages coming through from spirit, everyone is jostling me to get my attention, and sometimes I only pass messages on rather than reflect on them, as I would do in a one-to-one situation. Often, when I'm standing there in front of an audience, some very sensitive material comes through. I always say to people that they should hang on to the information as it's often only later, when things are quieter, that people recognise the relevance of what I've said. In the situation I had with Jacqueline it was slightly different in that I absolutely knew there was a child there. She was denying it but the spirit was adamant. I may get things wrong, but they don't, and her dad kept pushing it at me.

In situations where the recipient of the message isn't recognising it, I will say to spirit, 'She says "no"; give me something else.' They might then say, *'Ask her about the farm,'* or *'Remind her of that shell bracelet she had when she was little.'* All of this will help to spark memories in someone's mind – usually. With Jacqueline it just wasn't happening. Every time this man in spirit gave me something else to pass on, she refuted it. I was absolutely convinced that these signs were for her – but why would she be denying everything if she had made the effort to come to the show in the first place?

There have been occasions when I've been given very strong, clear messages from spirit that no one in the audience picks up. That's fine; it takes courage to put your hand up in front of everyone when you don't know what is going to come out. There are also cases where the person who was desperate to come to the show gets nothing, whereas the friend they've dragged along for company is the one who is recognised by spirit, but they don't want to talk. However, in this case I felt something else was happening. The message was for Jacqueline but she didn't want it and was being very defiant.

'Anyway, your dad wants me to tell you that everything is fine,' I said. 'He says that he's looking after your little boy and you mustn't worry about either of them.'

She shrugged and sat down, muttering to herself.

I resumed the rest of the show. By this time I was pretty sure what was going on. Jacqueline had been through a termination many years ago. I could almost feel her guilt emanating from where she was sitting in the audience and I knew I had been right not to push it. Admitting to something she still felt awful about, in front of all these strangers, would have been damaging for her.

It came as no surprise to me when I saw someone hanging around in the car park at the end of the evening when the show was over.

Jacqueline stood there, a lone figure in the car park. 'Can I talk to you?' she asked, shakily. 'In private?'

I knew that she was embarrassed to be there, given the way she had been during the show, but that didn't matter in the slightest to me.

'Of course you can,' I said, quickening my step to meet her and giving her a hug. 'Of course you can. Shall we go for a coffee?'

'What you said,' she began, 'I think I know what you meant – but I can't understand it. I can't get my head around it.'

I held her as she started to cry.

'I did a terrible thing,' she wept.

'No, no, you didn't,' I reassured her. 'You did what you had to do.'

'You don't know – you don't know what I did,' she continued.

'I do know – remember, I saw your dad and he spoke with me. I know you had a termination. I know that you wanted your baby very much but that you just couldn't go through with it.'

She looked shocked. 'How can you possibly know all of that?' she asked.

'I just do,' I replied. 'What you need to know is that your baby is in spirit, he's a little boy, and his grandfather is looking after him. They're both happy and content. They both spend all their time together, and they both want you to know that they love you.'

'Are you sure? I've always felt so guilty. Are you just saying this to make me feel better?'

I'm asked that a lot, but take a moment to think about it. How could I have known this complete stranger had family links to certain places, that she had a father with the exact characteristics I'd described, that her father had told me her name, and that she'd had a termination? If she could believe the 'facts', why could she not also believe the rest of what her father had told me: that she was forgiven and all was well?

It was an emotional moment. Shocked and totally taken aback, Jacqueline listened as I told her that she could forgive herself completely. In floods of tears, she said that she now, at least, felt that she could move on with her life, knowing that the child was safe and loved.

Previously Jacqueline had been feeling as though she were guilty of killing her baby, but if she had understood the contract all souls make she wouldn't have thought that way. You have to allow yourself to move on.

What was touching about this story was the way in which, by looking after his grandson, Jacqueline's father was also looking after her. The links between children and parents continue even when one has passed. I got the impression that he hadn't been the best dad in the world on this plane because he was usually drunk, so he was paying some of his dues by being a fantastic grandfather and supporting his daughter from the other side. His words to me were, *'There were things I could never do then, but there are things I can do now to help.'*

I always say to people that they can do more up there than they ever managed down here. Of course, when you don't have the drink and distractions around you it's easier to be a good person and step up to your responsibilities. Many people get that balance only when they pass on. They finally get the chance to make up for things and create a beautiful lasting memory for their loved ones. I urge everyone to forgive themselves – as parents and as children themselves. You can't go back and change things that have passed.

The man with the shiny buttons

I've lost count of the number of times someone has said to me that their little ones have spoken accurately of ancestors who died long before they were born. They can describe both their characters and appearances. It doesn't surprise me in the least, but it can shock those left behind. Children, especially those who are spiritual and attuned to spirit, know so much.

One woman told me that her son kept saying he could see a man. She dismissed it for as long as she could – it's an easier option – but her son wouldn't give up. He would talk about the man, saying that the man was there, telling her what the man was doing. He called him Joe and chatted as if he knew him very well indeed. In particular, the little boy said that Joe had shiny buttons on his coat, and this was a point he kept repeating.

It wasn't until this had been going on for some time that it all fell into place when the woman decided to look into some family history and construct a family tree. She went around all her relatives collecting photos and find-ing out who was who. When she was given a photograph of her great-grandfather in his army uniform with shiny buttons, she was shocked to discover that he was called Joe.

Her little boy used to tell her that his granddad was singing and he would repeat some wartime songs in a drunken voice, obviously just copying what he could hear. There was no way a child would have known these songs – or that they were the favourites of his great-grandfather who had been brought up in wartime, and who liked a drink. The little boy often appeared to be in fits of laughter over nothing. When his mum asked what he was laughing at, he'd say it was 'the funny man carrying on'. This man was having fun and sharing good times with his great-grandchild, which I think is lovely. The little boy would sit for hours playing happily with no one that his mother could see, and he continued to talk about the happy man and sing his songs. It was very positive that the great-grandfather's energy was being passed on in this way and I'm sure that he also got a great deal from it. In life he would have been dismissed as someone who was always making a show of himself when he'd had a drink, but to his grandson he was just happy and funny. He would be more likely to be full of this fun anyway after he moved to spirit.

Positive and negative energy

If you have a crying baby who becomes settled in a particular room, or an anxious child who is comforted by a special area of your house, take these things as signs. If I had a crying baby who stopped when I took it to the corner of the spare room, I'd spend all my time there rather than avoiding it. This means there is positive energy in that place sent by someone in spirit, and you might find that your baby stares at it and laughs, even though you can't see anything there yourself. I'd put my chair there. Be guided by the child, and life will be much easier.

Television has contributed a lot of the negative views we have about anything to do with intuition and spiritual awareness – even the word 'psychic' has spooky connotations. When some people hear of children who can see and sense things, they immediately think, *Amityville Horror!* – but it isn't like that at all. I hate the word 'paranormal' because, to me, all of this is perfectly normal. When you think of where we came from, of how much our ancestors had to rely on intuition and their senses, it makes it all seem so much more acceptable, as it should be. The sixth sense is nothing to be scared of; it is just that – another sense – and as natural as seeing and touching.

It is true that children can't control things in the same way as adults, so there are times when they are more susceptible to 'bad' spirits or events that frighten them, but these can be explained and the fear minimised if common sense is used. In fact, there's very little to be scared of in terms of spirit, so try not to pass on your knee-jerk reactions to your children because, in doing so, you may be killing off their intuition. Instead, glory in their knowledge and gifts, and see what you can learn from them and from children who have passed to spirit too.

If your child grows up in an environment or household where spirit is seen positively, then he or she will attract positive spirit. If a child mentions angels or 'friends' and his parents respond by saying, 'How lovely that you have a friend,' or, 'Isn't that nice that someone is watching over you?' then good spirits will be drawn in. But if you are in an environment or household where everyone feels they are in the middle of a horror film as soon as spirit is mentioned, then that too becomes a self-fulfilling prophecy. You set yourself up for bad things.

The power of the mind is an amazing tool. When I was five years old and I saw the Angel of Death, it hadn't chosen me. That Angel was there, going about its business, and if anyone with psychic ability had been around they would have seen it. When I saw it, it wasn't focusing on me – I just caught whatever was happening.

Children are conditioned in every way, and matters to do with other planes are no different. If you tell them that ghosts and ghouls are nasty, evil creatures that will haunt them, they'll look for that and they'll believe it. When I started to work in this field, I had my own reservations. I still have my own fears. I would be terrified if anything dark or horrible presented itself to me. As a result I made a conscious choice not to work at that level. I decided not to and I kept things that way. I simply don't get anything like that coming through now. Any time a negative or 'bad' spirit has made an approach to me – and it has happened on a few rare occasions – I just say, 'I'm sorry, that's not for me.'

I remember one night I was talking to a man who was very keen on Wicca. He told me he was a medium, and the woman he was with leaned over and said, in a doom-laden voice, 'He gets *terrible* things – really awful, terrible things.' They were revelling in it. He started telling me about one spirit he couldn't get rid of who tormented the life out of him. He went on for ages, and the woman at his side was pitching in with her own despondent remarks.

At the end of their confession, I felt quite annoyed. 'I think you must attract it,' I told him. 'I've never had anything like that.'

He might have been upset by my attitude, but it was the truth. Listening to the way he was speaking, I wasn't surprised that he drew the bad stuff.

'I would never have anything like that,' I told him. 'I just don't go there.'

To be honest, I'd be too scared. Imagine going to your bed at night and not knowing what you were going to wake up to? No, thanks! Some people have very low energy and, if that's the case, it will be a matter of like attracting like. If you don't attract it and don't ask for it, you won't get it — but if you dwell on the bad side of spirit (if you dwell on the bad side of anything), it will come in droves. Birds of a feather flock together.

Children don't necessarily understand this, but they are conditioned by the environment and the adults around them. If they are around negativity and fear, that is what they will attract spiritually. All parents should want the best for their children. Just as you would teach them to cross roads safely, and how to read, so too can you pass on understanding about spiritual matters which will stand them in good stead throughout their time on this plane. Personally, I can't understand why anyone would want to miss out on this valuable aspect of their child's development.

Chapter 6

The bonds that do not weaken

When children pass, they often retain links to siblings, cousins and other children to whom they have been close, as well as to their parents. I've witnessed the continuing relationships between children who were close on the Earthly plane during many readings I've given and through many stories told by friends.

One woman, Val, told me that when she was young she used to see spirit all the time, but it was only when she was about eleven that she realised these people were ghosts and not just 'normal' visitors. Val asked her mother why there were ghosts in their house and her mum told her that both she and her grandmother saw these people too. Val got the impression that she was 'cursed', because her mother saw the visions as very negative and annoying.

'I used to pray to God to send them away,' she told Val. 'When you were three and your baby sister died, I would wake up in the middle of the night to find her bouncing on my mum's bed. I was horrified and just wanted it all to stop.'

Val couldn't accept this – she didn't want to see ghosts and it was only later in life that she came to understand this.

Soon after her marriage, Val's other sister, Kate, gave birth to twin boys, whom she called Allan and Thomas. Thomas was born with a serious heart condition and, despite having surgery throughout the first few years of his life, he passed away when he was three. Five years later, Kate gave birth to a daughter, Megan, but she never told her about her other sibling. As far as Megan knew, she had one big brother and that was it. When the little girl was about two and a half, Kate heard her chatting in another room one day. She listened at the door as the child laughed and giggled happily. When Kate went in and asked who was there, she said it was her brother. Kate was puzzled as she had already taken the boy to school.

'Allan will be in class by now. He left just after breakfast,' she said.

The little girl looked at her and said, 'No, silly. Not that brother – my other one. He says to tell you that he still loves you and wishes that you would talk to him. He says to tell you that "me" is here.'

This stunned Kate. When her other son, Thomas, had been on this plane, if ever anyone asked him his name, he would say 'me'. This convinced her that Megan was genuinely in touch with her son in spirit.

Since that day, Megan has continued to pass on messages from her Thomas. He hates to see his mother sad and is always urging her not to cry. One Christmas, Kate was crying outside the house, thinking about her lost son, and she heard her daughter coming down the steps to the garden. When she reached Kate, she asked, 'Why are you crying? It's Christmas and Thomas can't be with you all of the time. He's upstairs playing on the computer with his brother.' Kate realised that the reason why she had been feeling so down was that she had been feeling Thomas's absence acutely and that was probably because he wasn't there in spirit at that moment – he was busy doing other things.

For a while, Megan wasn't getting good marks at school because the fact that she was seeing spirit all the time made it hard to concentrate. Auntie Val stepped in and had a chat with her. She brought in the Angel Gabriel, the angel of healing and children, and asked him for help and guidance. They decided that he would take away the child's awareness of spirit for a while, and he did. It stopped until Megan was ready to cope with her gifts again.

Psychic abilities are often passed on through families like this, and can go back generations. Val is a medium, as is Megan, and so were Val's mother and grandmother. It means that when a child needs guidance there should be someone nearby who can give it.

Stacey and her sister

Once when I was doing a show in Essex a man who called himself 'Uncle Jed' came through with a message for 'Stacey'. Immediately a young girl called Stacey put her hand up and said that she did have an Uncle Jed who had passed. The messages started coming thick and fast. Uncle Jed wanted me to tell Stacey that she should have more confidence in her own skills and abilities in the career she had chosen (which was accountancy). There was a lot of general advice, and I suppose a cynic might say that it wasn't specific enough to be convincing, but Uncle Jed also had more pointed remarks to make.

'Tell her to watch her driving!' he cautioned, adding that she had recently been involved in an incident while driving. I passed this on to Stacey, and asked, 'So what happened?'

'You tell me!' she replied.

I tuned in to Uncle Jed again, who told me that his niece had bumped her car. Only the paint had been scratched, but it had been enough to give her a fright. Stacey was amazed that I could tell her this – it had been such a minor incident she'd forgotten all about it – and she promised to heed Jed's warning. He said she needed to slow down when she was driving, or the next incident would be fatal.

All of this was enough to make Stacey realise the link was genuine, so when Jed brought forward a boy of about six months I wasn't surprised that she recognised the little one straight away as her brother. Jed told me that the child had passed over due to smoke inhalation because he was in a house fire, and when I passed this on to Stacey she began to cry. She wasn't there at the time, but had been staying overnight with a friend. I could see that the fire had started in the kitchen. A chip pan had caught on fire, and before anyone knew it the house was in flames.

I could feel the guilt of the parents through Stacey, and sensed that they had become very reclusive as the years passed as a result of this terrible accident; again, Stacey confirmed this. Uncle Jed told Stacey to let her parents know that it had been too long and they must stop blaming themselves. He became very emotional as he talked about the way the family had become dysfunctional after the passing of Stacey's brother. Stacey's parents had caused a lot of damage to their relationship with her by focusing on what had happened and the son they lost, rather than caring for the child who stayed behind on this plane. Their life with their daughter was ruined.

A lot of this information was coming through Jed from Stacey's brother, whom Jed now cared for, but he didn't feel that he could communicate with me directly. He felt responsible for the way their parents had treated

Stacey, and he preferred to pass everything on through Jed. This boy desperately wanted to convey his love for his sister, but was worried that Stacey would feel resentful towards him because he had become the sole focus of their parents' attention. Of course she didn't harbour any such feelings. Jed urged Stacey to tell her parents everything she had heard in the hope that they could move on with their lives at last and learn to appreciate the remarkable young woman who was still in their family.

The brother who had died made it very clear that he felt an incredibly strong link to Stacey, despite the distance between the two planes they were on. Those in spirit can only progress so far if we on this plane are holding them back, and Stacey's parents were guilty of this. They were stuck in the past and simply couldn't get over the tragedy that had occurred to them. Stacey was almost invisible to them, which was another tragedy. The terribly sad thing about this for me was how awful it must have been for Stacey to play second fiddle to a child who wasn't even here any more. How do you compete with a ghost? She more or less had to bring herself up because her parents' emotions were tied up in the son they had lost.

To be honest, I don't know whether telling them this would have made any difference, and I don't know whether Stacey did, but I do think the reading made her realise that none of it was her fault. It gave her recognition as a person and put her childhood in context. There was love there for her, but it came from her brother, not her mum and dad. She told me that it was a relief to have someone, an objective observer, look at all of this and say, 'It's okay, it's not you.'

My sister Rita

The sadness of Stacey's story took me back to my own childhood. I always had to push myself forwards to make myself visible because my parents just couldn't 'see' me. If they asked my sister Rita to go and get something for them, I'd be there and back before she'd even stood up. I would do the shopping, make the beds, clean the house, and all I was really doing was asking, in my head, *'Can you see me?'* But they couldn't. It's only while writing this that I can understand why I relate so strongly to stories in which children are treated in the way I was, and in which spirit tries to help them to move on.

It was a different era when I was young. You got on with life and concentrated on the practical, but I never felt that I was relevant. I know my dad didn't want children, so perhaps when I came along there was resentment. I never asked. Maybe by the time Rita arrived he had accepted fatherhood a little more, because I remember him treating her like a new toy. Just recently she mentioned what a great relationship she'd had with my dad, and I was taken aback. It was so different for me. I don't think he really knew how to cope as a parent; he certainly never showed affection. I only really got to know him in the last three years of his life. Before that, I hadn't even realised that he had a sense of humour. Rita can't understand that as she found him funny all the time. I sometimes wonder if we lived in separate houses! To me, Dad was cold and I don't think he could have got much enjoyment from life. I believe his own childhood was devoid of emotion and warmth and that could explain why he was the way he was. He was the same as a grandfather with my kids.

I was always close to Rita, though. We have a strong and deep bond. I never felt any resentment towards her but I did feel alone as a child, and that I didn't fit in. In some ways I still feel like that, but I'm comfortable with it now. When you are shy and quiet and timorous, it is difficult and there are repercussions. I can totally sympathise with children who feel invisible. With Stacey, I could see that her brother was still trying to look out for her, even though he had passed over. It wasn't her brother's fault, in the same way that none of the problems in my childhood were my sister's fault. Brothers and sisters usually interact on a deep level, even when they are being treated differently, because they link into an energy, an invisible sense that takes over.

Luke and Andrew

Siblings who have passed often try to protect those who have been left behind, and I came across a moving example of this when I did a reading for a young man called Luke. I was soon made aware of the presence of a younger boy in spirit, one who was about twelve years old.

'Luke,' I said, 'I have your brother here – Andrew is with me.' I told Luke that I knew Andrew had passed as the result of a road accident, and that he wanted his big brother to know he was all right. What I was receiving from Andrew made me feel that he was a very grounded child, and that he liked things to be based in practicalities.

'*Tell Luke about his chest and about the roof,*' he kept saying.

I passed on these words, but told Andrew that I needed a bit more.

'*He has a chest infection and needs to get it looked at. He thinks doctors are all the same; he hates them, but he must go see one. I'm worried about him and I want him to get checked out.*'

I gave Luke these words and he smiled. 'He's right,' he said, 'I *do* hate doctors and I *do* think they're all the same. I'll go, though, if he wants me to. I'll do as I'm told.'

This made Andrew happy, and he said to me, '*I'm on a roll! Tell him about the roof now! I know that it's leaking and he thinks that builders and plumbers are as untrustworthy as doctors! He needs to get the roof and his chest fixed. It's so like him to leave everything until the last minute.'*

Luke said he would get it seen to but I sensed it would take more for him to understand the urgency of Andrew's message.

Andrew became agitated. *'He has to get his chest looked at! It's really important – forget the roof, just get to a doctor.'*

He seemed worried that there was something seriously wrong now. I asked Andrew if there was anything he could tell me that would convince Luke this was all absolutely genuine and that his words should be heeded.

'Yes,' came the reply. *'Remind him of this. When we were little, we used to steal potatoes from a farm close to where we lived. He'll remember that.'*

Luke did remember and said he'd never expected that to come up. He started laughing and I could see that he was touched by the memory. It's beautiful when siblings can still share memories even though one of them has passed.

'Andrew would always look out for me,' he told me, 'even though I was older than him. It looks as though nothing has changed. I'll go to the doctor, Andrew; I'll make an appointment tomorrow.'

Luke left feeling very uplifted. A few days later he called me to say that he had been to see his GP and had been told that he had a very serious chest infection which could have turned into pneumonia had he left it any longer. Laughing, he said that his little brother would love being right – and that I should pass on the news that someone was coming to look at his roof the following week too!

Moira's cousin

These continuing links between siblings and family members cross all boundaries. It doesn't matter whether the family was small or large, or even whether the people concerned seemed close when they were both on the Earthly plane. When I read for a lovely lady called Moira I was again touched by the evidence of a love that continues no matter what.

Moira was very nervous to begin with. I asked her if she had ever had a reading before, and wasn't surprised when she said that she had not. I reassured her that I wouldn't pass on anything that might upset her and she relaxed slightly.

I began by telling Moira I was hearing from spirit about a recent conflict with some work colleagues. She was very worried by all the arguing that was happening and didn't know how to put things right. I told her that this situation was actually representative of something more deep-rooted in her life. She lived her life doing what she thought others wanted her to do rather than what she wanted herself. She nodded at this.

'I am sensing this is how you got into the dispute in the first place,' I told her, 'and you need to learn a lesson from it.' I knew this all made sense and should act as the proof Moira needed to accept I was genuinely in communication with spirit. However, the message I was receiving which mattered more than anything was coming from a little baby girl who had passed.

I told Moira that I could see a little girl and that she was waiting to communicate. Her eyes filled up as I asked her permission to proceed, and she nodded.

'It was a passing many years ago, wasn't it?' I asked, and she confirmed this. 'What are you feeling so guilty about?'

'It was my fault,' she said, as the tears started to fall. 'It was all my fault.'

I didn't see how this could be. From what I was getting, I could tell that Moira herself had been very young when the baby had passed. All of a sudden, the child who was in spirit clearly told me, *No, it wasn't her fault, she must know it wasn't her fault, she was only a child.*

This baby's energy was very uplifting, very positive. There was a real sense of smiling about her, and it was hard to sense any upset at all. She showed me an image of a baby – her – in a cot, and of a little girl of about six years old (whom I assumed to be Moira) playing in a different room. The next image showed both children but also a woman in the scene – a screaming woman.

Sometimes I get the correct message, but I don't know the context, so Moira explained it all to me.

'I was staying with my Auntie Fee,' she began, 'who had a little baby of a few months old. Auntie Fee needed to run to the local shop to get something. It was only a stone's throw away and she asked if I would stay in the house with the baby. The baby had been sleeping for ages and it was raining outside, so Auntie Fee didn't want to drag us all out and she'd only be away for five minutes, so it seemed fine.'

Moira was getting more and more upset as she went on, but the child in spirit was sending out comforting energy which would eventually break through and reach her.

'Go on,' I encouraged, feeling it was important she got it all out.

'When Auntie Fee came back, she went upstairs immediately to check on the baby. I had been downstairs in the living room the whole time, just playing. I heard screaming. It went through my bones and it wouldn't stop. I went upstairs to the baby's nursery and Auntie Fee was standing there, holding the baby and rocking backwards and forwards. The baby was dead.' Moira was in pieces by this stage. 'I should have checked. I should have checked.'

Clearly, none of this was her fault. She had only been six years old, and even if she had gone up to check there was nothing she could have done. Her cousin was keen for her to be made aware of the fact that she had stopped breathing long before her mother had even left the house.

I found it terribly sad that Moira had allowed her whole life to be defined by this one tragedy. She had never got over it and had led a life where she always thought of others and never recognised her own needs. She had never married and had become almost a recluse as the years went on, feeling that she could never make up for something she should never have blamed herself for in the first place. The cousin in spirit now wanted her to release herself from this terrible pain.

Moira cried for some time and I sat there with her – as did her cousin. However, when she stopped there was a brightness about her that hadn't been there when she first arrived.

'I've carried this with me all my life,' she said. 'Auntie Fee never blamed me, but I blamed myself. Is it true? Was I really not at fault? Was there nothing I could have done?'

Of course there wasn't. I consoled her as best I could, and passed on as much of her cousin's energy as possible. When she left, Moira told me that she felt as if she could begin to live a little. I knew that it would take a while for her to get all of this processed in her mind, but the spirit child had allowed her a glimmer of hope.

Owen and Mark

When I did a reading for a man called Owen who had recently lost his mother, it wasn't his mother who came forward but a boy called Mark, his little brother who had passed away at the age of four. When I told Owen that Mark was there, he was delighted.

'I've always felt the loss of him,' he said.

'But you shouldn't have,' I told him. 'He's always been there.'

Mark had passed due to an inherited genetic condition when his big brother was six. He had been in a lot of pain, but he was a cheeky, happy wee thing, both then and now. Even in spirit, I could tell he was always up to mischief and full of fun.

'He used to get in trouble!' Mark told me, pointing at Owen. *'He was really naughty and always getting a row!'*

Owen was embarrassed by this, but I told him that I only passed on the messages, didn't judge their content.

Mark came in again to tell me, *'He got in really bad trouble once, you know. The police came to find him.'*

I passed that on to Mark, and he was stunned. 'How did you know that?'

I told him that his brother was dropping him in it by giving me a detailed account of his past misdemeanours. It would be quite wrong of me to mention any more of them in print! Owen was beginning to get upset and I think Mark realised that although he was only trying to be playful he had gone too far. He left for a while as I tried to convince Owen that it didn't matter to me in the slightest, but then Mark returned – with their mum. Owen broke down completely. His mum didn't say very much – she wasn't that type of person – but she sent him so much love that it was an amazing feeling to be part of. It was a very beautiful moment.

Mark had done well. He was instrumental in helping their mother to come through for his brother, and he tried to do it with humour, fun and love – even if he did give me a bit too much information.

All of these people – and the many more whose stories I haven't had space to tell in this book – have found out that what we experience on this plane only explains love to a certain degree. It may be a cliché, but love never dies – and clichés are often the most accurate of all sayings. It may be that you have 'lost' someone yourself but, like Iona and Daniel, you have felt as if they are still here. That's because they are. They haven't been lost; they are just waiting for you to find them again, and it will be a beautiful day when you do.

Chapter 7

The comfort they bring

Some psychics believe that children only possess psychic abilities at certain stages of their lives, whether on this plane or another, but I have twenty-seven years of experience to prove the opposite. I've found that there is no limit to the age at which a child can communicate and that they have many different ways of bringing comfort and support to those they love. I've come across many examples of this, but one of the most memorable happened in Birmingham, during one of my shows.

As usual before a show, I spent the day tuning in and putting out 'feelers' to let spirit know that I was ready to take messages for any of their loved ones who would be there that evening. This is always a very exciting time for me as I never know who I'm going to get. As soon as I sent out the open invitation, a little boy came through. His name was Carl and he was about eight years old. He had a beautiful smile, the sort that lights up a room. What was surprising about Carl was that he didn't have anything to say when he made himself known to me.

Throughout the day he walked beside me, he never left my side, but not a word was uttered. Carl kept looking up at me every time I glanced his way but I just left him to it, smiling when we caught each other's eye. I knew he would communicate when he was ready.

Just before I left the hotel for the venue, Carl smiled at me once more, then I got the most awful feeling. Suddenly I knew exactly how Carl had died because I was feeling it, and it was one of my worst nightmares – the little one had drowned. As with deaths which have involved drink, drugs or choking, I experience all the sensations associated with fatal drownings. It would be very easy to panic – and, to be honest, there have been times when I have – but I try to retain an awareness that it will pass, and that through feeling what the child has felt I may be given valuable evidence which will prove to their parent, sibling or other loved one that they genuinely are making contact. In the wider scheme of things it is a small price to pay, but I can't deny that I dread it.

As the drowning sensation passed, Carl began to communicate and he told me that he wanted his mummy to know that he was there. I said that I would tell her if she was at the show, but Carl shook his head and laughed again.

'I want her to know the actual times when I am there doing things,' he told me.

'What do you mean?' I asked.

'I play tricks on them. I play tricks on Mum and everyone else, but no one seems to realise it's me!' Carl was giggling as he told me this and I got the impression of a very happy, very playful little boy.

I encouraged him, as he seemed to be having a good time. 'What do you get up to?' I asked. 'What tricks do you play?'

'I turn the lights on, then I turn them off. If they're watching telly, I make it flicker, then when they get up I sort it! I turn the dimmer lights down, then when they walk over I turn them back up again. I blow little breezes, I move things, I hide things. But they never seem to know it's me.'

'Do you worry that you'll get into trouble?' I asked him.

'No!' he flashed back. *'I want them to know it's me. I want them to know I'm there.'* He went quiet for a moment. *'I really, really want them to know I'm there.'*

It was very touching. He was a lovely little boy and, although he had a full awareness that he had passed, he still seemed to want and need that link and recognition with his family, with his mum especially.

'Shall I tell your mum?' I asked.

'Yes! Yes, please!'

When the show began that night, Carl was there immediately.

'Mum's here!' he said. *'Mum's here!'*

I felt his excitement, so I ignored all the other spirits who were clamouring to pass on messages to their own loved ones, and asked for Carl's mum first of all.

'I'm sorry for not giving everyone a chance to settle,' I began, 'but I have a little boy here who is really anxious to contact his mum.'

There was a murmur of anticipation. There are so many people hoping for messages, and when I make very general introductions like this I suppose their hopes are raised.

'This little boy is very beautiful, very happy, with a lovely smile,' I said, and gave a few more details such as his age and some personal details that would identify the family, which I can't repeat here for reasons of privacy. It is important not to rush into contact too quickly so as to be sure I get the right person, and also to let them settle a little into realising something amazing is about to happen.

'It's Carl,' I said. 'I have little Carl coming through.'

One woman put her hand up and the microphone was passed to her.

'I think it might be for … I knew a Carl,' she said.

'You still do,' I encouraged. 'He's here.'

'Just now?' the woman asked.

'Yes,' I confirmed. 'I know that you have a connection with him, but Carl wants to pass on a message to her mum. That's not you, is it?'

The woman shook her head and looked at her companion on the next seat. I knew she was Carl's mum, but I also knew that she was scared of talking to me. It can be too much for some people, even though it's what they came for. 'I'm a friend of Carl's mum,' said the first woman. 'This is his mum.'

'All right,' I said, talking to the mum. 'I know that this may seem an awful lot to take in, but there's more. If you need me to prove that I am communicating with your wee laddie, I can do that. Are you ready?'

She nodded, but she looked terrified. I gave her lots of details, which Carl was passing to me, largely through pictures and feelings, and I finished by telling her what her son was saying over and over again.

'*I so wanted to speak to her today. I so wanted to speak to her today.*'

Both women had gasped in shock many times at what I passed on, but when I told them that today was very important, Carl's mum burst into tears.

'It's my birthday,' she said. 'He always loved birthdays and loved celebrating them together.'

'He still does,' I said. 'He still wants to.'

'But he isn't here any more,' his mum whispered.

'He is! He's here with me now, and he wants me to tell you that he is with you often; you just haven't been putting two and two together.'

'What do you mean?' Carl's mum asked, confused.

I told her about the tricks with the lights, about Carl hiding items, about all the little things he did to make his presence felt, and his mum started to smile through the tears.

'I've never got over the loss of him,' she said, 'but you're right. I have actually thought at times that it might be him, but I've never let myself dare to hope for too long that it might be true.' She started to cry.

When people are upset, I always ask if they want me to stop, but Carl's mum said that they were tears of joy at the fact that she was finally in direct contact with her little boy. I was able to pass on the information that there were four other family members in the spirit world with Carl, looking after him, and this comforted the woman hugely. It was a very emotional start to the night.

As I stood on stage that night, Carl was showing me lots of ways in which he was 'naughty' – but of course it wasn't really naughty behaviour at all. He showed me a little picture sitting on a shelf and then shifting sideways. He showed me lights being put on and off and flickering. He showed me things being hidden and then brought out again later and placed elsewhere. It is quite easy for spirit to move physical things. It happens all the time; even adult spirits do it.

I once did a reading for a woman who was desperate to contact her son and to have evidence that he was still around. I said to her, 'You know all of those times you put something down but when you came back it was gone?' She nodded. 'You know all of those times when you went back to the first place you thought it was to begin with and it *was* there even though you know you checked?' She nodded again. 'You know all of those times when you thought you were going mad because objects seemed to be getting moved around and you *know* you didn't do it and you *know* there had been no one else in the house?' She nodded again, and started to smile a little. 'Well, who do you think was doing it? How much more evidence do you need that your son is still here? He's playing jokes on you every single day!'

I think most people will relate to that. Reflect on the number of times you've put your car keys or house keys or bank card or gloves or remote control down in a specific place. You get up to make a cup of tea or go to the loo, then return, and the keys or remote or whatever has gone. But you *know* where you left the missing item, don't you? So you then search all around that place, under the cushions, behind the curtains, everywhere. You leave the room, even though you *know* the keys or remote couldn't have walked out by themselves. You give up. You sit down, get frustrated, get up for one last look in the place where you first expected the thing to be – and where you have definitely looked already – and there it is! You're not going mad. You're just the target of a practical joke from spirit. No one ever sees it. How wonderful it would be to catch them at it! I bet there is evidence on CCTV somewhere and we don't even know it, because if no one is looking for it in the first place it goes undetected.

There is a mischievousness within a lot of spirit, and Carl certainly had it in spades. In life, he would have been that sort of prankster. He was a lovely boy, full of joy, and he gave me his happiness, his cheekiness, but there was a serious note as well. His parents weren't there when he died, and they carried a lot of guilt about it. He very much wanted to tell them that he was fine, and that by playing his little tricks he was trying to contact them.

I've had many, many cases of children passing when they have been alone and their parents have had no time to say 'goodbye'. I don't know whether having that time would make the slightest bit of difference, but the suddenness and unexpectedness of the loss hits very hard, and the feeling that the parent wants to connect with the child again and apologise is very strong. A bereaved parent who feels that they did not protect their child well enough is lost; they feel that they failed in the most basic of parental responsibilities and often just want to say how sorry they are. When protectiveness and guilt are combined, there is a powerful level of grief, which those who have passed try to soothe. The comfort is there if we are willing to accept it. They want us to know that, while they are no longer on our plane, they are still around. If death were the end, how would I even get these messages in the first place? A medium's job, primarily, is to let people know that there is something after *this*; that is why giving proof is so important. A medium is not there to tell fortunes.

The most important part of my job lies in providing proof and evidence of an after-life by clicking into the personality and events that happened in a person's life, and that is exactly what I'm doing. When I do a show I'm often visiting a part of the country where I have never been before and where I know no one. I laugh when conspiracy theorists suggest that mediums all travel with 'staff' who scour the local papers for weeks before they arrive, memorising the death notices, and staking out the homes of those who have lost loved ones. I wish I had the money to do that! Others have suggested that we place assistants in the theatre box offices and instruct them to follow people who buy tickets and build up a picture of their lives. Or we place 'spies' in the audience to listen in on what people are saying and then feed it back to us on stage. It all sounds very glamorous, and sometimes I wish my life was a high-tech spy thriller, but the truth is more boring and more wonderful than any of that. I am simply given information by spirit – maybe they are my spies! I don't have a vast army of staff, nor do I have high-level surveillance equipment tracking the every move of those who come to see me; I'm just a very normal woman who can pass on messages of comfort.

Even if I did spend a week in every city before a show, reading the newspapers and looking out for stories, how would I know the people concerned would be in the audience? Even if I read of a shooting and knew the victim's girlfriend was in the audience, how could I describe his personality, tell her what he liked for his supper or what his favourite colour was? How could I tell her things that had happened to him when he was a toddler, things she didn't even know, and that she had to check with his mother to find out that they were accurate? Where does all of that stuff come from? If someone is a true cynic, I'll never change their mind – and, actually, that's not what I'm here for. I'm here to help those who are open to being helped, to being comforted. I'm here to prove that there is something beyond this. If you want to believe along with me, that's great – but if you don't want to, that's great as well, because the world would be a dull place if everyone agreed with each other.

Over the last decade or so more and more people are looking into spiritual matters, partly because the world is in such a state of crisis that they feel lost and want advice on the way forward. Some things never change, no matter what's happening with the government or the economy, and connecting with the spirit world gives a sense of continuity and security to all of us. I have often seen people who, having come to me for comfort when they have lost someone, are so blown away by the messages they receive that they want to develop their own spiritual awareness and learn still more. That bridge is very important.

Some critics claim that mediums exploit the vulnerable at a difficult time in their lives, but I would respond by asking how I can be exploiting them by giving peace of mind through evidence-based messages. What is the difference between that and counselling? I'd also point out that not everyone gets contact. It's not a direct telephone line; I can make no guarantees. If I was in the business of exploitation, everyone who came to me would get miraculous messages, albeit very generalised ones. If you don't get a message, it doesn't mean that spirit isn't with you. It might not be the right time or you may not be ready to hear it.

Recently a woman came for a Tarot reading and I could get nothing. When this happens I always put the cards out twice. If I still don't get anything I tell them to come back in a week. This woman had lost her mum a few weeks earlier and, as an only child, felt completely lost. She and her mum had been everything to each other. Although this woman was in her fifties, she had still been her mum's 'little girl'. I honestly felt she wasn't ready for a reading, and told her so. It would have upset her and wouldn't have been in her best interests. It wouldn't have been fair of me to push it, and I told her that when the time was right the information would still be there and she would be in a much better place to receive it. She needed to look after herself first, and find her way on this plane without her mum. In some ways she was still a child, and she needed to be in a much stronger place before she started communicating with spirit.

A girl called Janie

When a child in spirit feels strongly that they want to communicate through me, or any other medium, we will then try to 'hunt down' the person they want to speak with. Some years ago, when I first began to do readings, I went to see a group of women in a house in Dundee. When I arrived, there were two children, a boy and a girl, playing in the kitchen. One of the women, Mary, told them to go upstairs as she wanted to use the kitchen for the session. The little girl was hers, and the boy belonged to another woman there who wanted a reading. The little girl lingered behind even when Mary chivvied her along. She went to check on the little boy and she hung around, never taking her eyes off me.

'Hello,' I said. 'What's your name?'

'Janie.'

'What age are you, Janie?'

'Six.'

She wasn't saying much but she clearly wanted to be there. I started laying out the cards and she became much more inquisitive.

'What are they?' she enquired.

'They're cards which help me look at things. They tell me stories about people.'

'Why do you need them to tell you things about people?' Janie asked.

'I can talk to people who aren't beside us any more, and the cards help me.'

She thought about that for a moment. 'Are they dead? Are you talking to dead people?'

I laughed at her bluntness. 'I don't really use that word, but I suppose they are.'

'If they're not alive, they're dead,' said Janie. 'But you haven't answered my question – why do you need the cards to tell you about people?'

'I did answer it!' I told her.

'No, you didn't. You told me that you talk to dead people, but I want to know how the cards help you do that. If anyone has your cards, can they talk to them?'

'No, they can't,' I answered.

'It's you who does the talking, not the cards. So why do you need the cards?'

These were great questions; she was a wise wee soul. 'To be honest, I don't need them. It makes other people feel better to have something to look at while I'm passing on messages from …'

'… dead people,' Janie finished.

'If I just sat and looked at folk while I was telling them what their granny was saying, they'd be a bit uncomfortable, wouldn't they? Cards help. But I don't need them really.'

Janie had wangled the truth out of me. The cards are not without purpose. They can help the psychic to focus and they are also a useful springboard to another realm. I often feel that they aid my intuitiveness and help me dive into the deep, but if I was stuck on a desert island with no cards I could still do what I do.

Janie spoke up again. 'I know stuff about people too.'

I had suspected as much. 'That's brilliant,' I told her.

'No. No, it's not,' she replied. 'No one listens to me, no one believes me.'

Just as she said that, her mother came back in and shooed her upstairs. Janie looked back at me as she left, and I so wanted to reach out to that little girl.

'Who do you want to start with?' she asked me.

'You, Mary,' I said. 'Let's start with you.'

After what had just happened, that seemed by far the most appropriate way to go about things. I gave her quite a straightforward reading as she was very easy to link into. To be honest, I had my own agenda, which may not have been the most professional way to go about things, but I desperately wanted to speak to her about Janie.

First of all, I told Mary that I could see she couldn't make her mind up whether to move house or stay put, and that she changed her mind most days. She confirmed all of this. I also told her that she had lost money some time during the last month, which again she agreed with. Then I got to the part I was really interested in: I started to speak about her two children – Janie and an older son Henry who wasn't there that day.

'Your eldest boy is a real joker, isn't he?' I said. She laughed immediately. 'He doesn't care what other folk think about him; he's just himself. You can take him or leave him, but he won't change for anyone.'

'You're spot on there,' she said. 'I can't believe you're getting all of this so quickly.'

'Now, Janie …' I began. 'Your other child is very different to her big brother.' I paused. 'She's psychic.'

'No!' she shouted. 'No! She's just a child. I don't want to hear this. Tell me more about the house move.'

'Mary,' I said, 'it is very important to hear this. In fact, it may be the reason you asked me to come here in the first place even though you weren't aware of it.'

'No, that isn't right – I just wanted to have a laugh. I don't want you saying these things,' she said, quietly.

It was obvious to me that she knew what I was saying was true, but she didn't want to face up to it. All of her prejudices and fears were coming to the fore. I didn't mind the fact that she had only seen my reading as a 'laugh' but it bothered me that she was blind to the way she could help her younger child if she was only willing to learn.

'Children can be psychic,' I told her, trying to be patient. 'I know what Janie has been like.'

'You can't, you can't even begin to imagine what it's been like.'

'I know that she has always come out with things that she couldn't have possibly known.'

Mary stopped to think. 'I suppose she does – but she may have overheard me talking.'

I wanted to ask whether they talked a lot about people who had passed over long before she was born. Did they talk about their thoughts and emotions with a six-year-old girl? 'I know that there was a time when she told you about a ring that you lost years ago – when you were pregnant with her.'

Mary almost fell off her chair. 'God, that's right,' she said, and I could see the penny starting to drop, if only very vaguely. 'What should I do about it?' she whispered.

'Nothing,' I said, 'except listen to her and at least let her know you believe her.' I felt this would bring about a revelation for both Mary and Janie. It could be a night that would change their relationship for the better, and forever.

There is much comfort to be gained from wonderful children like Janie, and they are generous with what they are willing to share. However, we must do our bit as well. By denying or ridiculing them we do them an injustice, and we risk missing out on so much.

Brenda and Liam

During a reading, it is often the tiniest details that really hit home and bring the biggest comfort. I was reminded of this when I did a reading for a lady called Brenda, in Newcastle. To begin with, I was contacted by Brenda's father, a very strong man to whom everyone paid attention. He was a man with presence and a clear sense of right and wrong. When I passed this on to Brenda, she was very emotional about it, but I could sense there was someone else there. While I was communicating with Brenda's father, there was another presence in the background and, while I was passing on the message to her, again, there was a boy waiting. I finished what I was telling Brenda, then asked the boy what he wanted to say. He told me that he was her son, Liam, and that he had passed a few years ago. He showed me an image of his death and I got a shocking pain in my chest and a tight feeling in my neck.

I informed Brenda about all of this and she let out a cry.

'That's my boy,' she whispered. 'That's my boy.'

Liam had been at his parents' house for the day and had gone home after his dinner. A couple of hours later his mum called him at the flat to make sure that he had arrived safely. It doesn't matter what age they are, you still feel that need to check, don't you? He wasn't answering the landline or his mobile, so she left it, thinking he'd maybe met a friend on the way back and gone out for a quick drink. Later that night one of Liam's friends called his parents' house. 'He's gone back to his own flat,' she told the boy. 'He left just after dinner.'

'That's funny,' said his friend. 'I've been trying to get him on both phones, but he isn't picking up.'

Brenda suggested that he might have gone for a drink, but the friend pointed out that Liam would have taken his mobile. As he said this, Brenda felt a knot in her stomach. Liam had charged the phone while he was at her house, and this boy was right – he always carried it with him and he always answered (they'd had many dinner-table arguments about that over the years).

The boy said he'd pop round to Liam's flat and check that he was all right, and promised to tell him to give his mum a ring. When he got there there was a light on, but Liam didn't answer the door. As the friend looked through the letterbox he could see Liam lying on the floor. It transpired that he had suffered a massive heart attack almost as soon as he returned to the flat. That's why I had felt the pain in my chest area when he had shown me his passing.

No one could have foreseen this, and Brenda was faced with the awful shock of the sudden loss of her beloved son. She was in two minds about what I was telling her now. I had passed on a huge amount of detail, all of which had come from Liam, but I could see that she still wasn't sure whether to believe me. Liam could tell that she was very upset and told me to emphasise that he was full of fun, and that he hadn't changed. He sent images of himself playing air guitar, which is exactly how he wants her to remember him, and before he left he sent me one more thing.

'Give Mum a bunch of flowers from me,' he requested, smiling.

'Any particular kind?' I asked, fully aware that Brenda was listening to me talking into 'thin air'.

'Oh yes!' Liam laughed. 'They have to be irises that have still to open!'

I knew as soon as he mentioned these very specific flowers that this would be the most powerful message for Brenda. She told me that irises were the only type of flower Liam ever bought her and that she still thought of him every time she saw them in a supermarket or florist's. The blooms were a connection between mother and son, and they helped to make it real for her.

It is often the case that some seemingly trivial detail is the one that provides proof positive. I'm often standing there thinking, 'I've given you all of that amazing other information, and it's a *hair clip* that has done it for you!' Everything clicks into place after that. Brenda was in floods of tears, but so happy that she had made contact.

It is in the minutiae of family life that people often find the most comfort, and if I can help to pass it on I am delighted to do so.

Chapter 8

Crystal children

I have met many wonderful children on the Earth plane and on the other side, and among the most fascinating of them are 'crystal children', a group of highly evolved souls who have been put on this earth to help change the planet. They are a fairly new race with a deep sense of wisdom, who are here to promote peace and understanding. I have used the phrase 'old souls' a lot in this book, and it applies to these children in particular. They don't like to conform to the rules of society, and may even rebel against it in later years – this makes them mavericks in their own way – but their intuition and psychic skills are highly tuned, and when they are at the crystal child stage they are warm and caring individuals whom it is a joy to be around.

Crystal children tend to be aged between newborn (isn't that remarkable?) and seven years old. Sometimes their gifts are lost before the age of seven if they aren't cultivated, but if they continue to progress from this age, they become 'indigo children'. I'll talk about them in chapter 10.

Crystal children are psychic and very sensitive, but frequently misunderstood. In order to fulfil the higher purpose for which they have been sent here, they are often even-tempered and fast, they jump around between a hundred subjects at once and want to know everything. As a result they may be diagnosed as having behavioural problems such as attention deficit hyperactivity disorder (ADHD) or attention deficit disorder (ADD). In their early years crystal children are quite laid back, but perhaps frustration with the workings of the world changes their attitudes as they get a little older.

Whenever I meet crystal children, I am aware of the way our society tends to label them. It isn't uncommon during a reading for someone to tell me about the 'problems' they are having with their toddler or young child. Perhaps the parents of crystal children are more likely to contact a medium for a reading because they are open-minded, and thus more likely to have a child with intuitive talents. Perhaps once I am in their environment the parent is encouraged by the energy the spirits bring and finds him or herself talking about matters that they didn't intend to discuss. Maybe it is something the child facilitates in a way none of us understands. I don't have the answer, but I am fascinated by the frequency with which the subject comes up.

Whatever is behind it, there are common worries. I'll be told of a child who has a delay in his speech, so that they don't talk as well or as much as their friends. I'll hear tales of children who say nothing at all when they're at home, but who are perfectly happy and content. Invariably, as she tells me these things, the mother will say, 'It's not a problem, really.'

'That's good,' I'll reply. 'It's probably just best to leave your child to progress at their own pace.'

There will be a bit of hesitation, then a few remarks about what 'people' have said. Other children talk more fluently, or with a larger vocabulary, or less haltingly.

'So, if your little one doesn't talk,' I'll say, playing devil's advocate, 'I take it that they don't get anything they want or need?'

'What do you mean?'

'I take it they never get a drink when they need one, or a biscuit? You won't know if they have a sore tummy or need a nap, will you? You won't know if they understand their bedtime story or the DVD you watch together? You won't know their likes and dislikes – in fact, you won't know anything about them if they can't communicate with you.'

'Oh, they can communicate!' I'll be assured. 'They just don't talk.'

'Right … so how do they do that?'

A whole list will be related. Singing songs (musical ability tends to be advanced in crystal children as music is often more interesting to them than the spoken word). Drawing diagrams. Sign language. And what every parent of one of these children describes as 'just letting me know'. And do *you* know what they mean by this? Mind reading. That's what it is. They communicate in a hundred different ways, few of them using verbal spoken cues, and these include the power of the mind. The irony is that when parents try to explain what they mean they find words inadequate – which is exactly the 'problem' their children are having! The mind-to-mind communication that exists between crystal children and those who love them goes beyond educational trends and Ofsted reports, but still everyone wants these precious little souls to fit in, even when this fitting in is against all of their best interests. It breaks my heart to see them squashed into regulatory boxes when they should be free to fly.

Let me ask you to stop for a moment and think of three things.

First of all, how often have you heard someone ask of a young child, 'Is he speaking yet?' It has become a measure of how intelligent a child is, and we all seem to want our children to adhere to structured ideals of intelligence. If you are a parent who has had to answer 'not yet' when your child is two or three, you will be met with sympathy and shock, and that starts to worry you. Never mind that you know everything your little one wants and needs – a stranger thinks it isn't right! Now, think of a child you know who has been a late developer with language. I bet that child is one of the cleverest souls you know.

The second thing I'd like you to consider is the rise in the number of diagnoses for conditions such as autism and Asperger's syndrome. Those of us who are forty-plus will be hard-pushed to recall any child of our generation who was labelled in such a way. Nowadays, is there anyone who doesn't know a child who has been tagged with a label like this? Can there really be 'new' conditions? Or is it that, when faced with things we don't understand, labels make us feel safer? We no longer have to deal with a child who doesn't fit into our narrow conceptions of 'normal'; we can say that they are 'suffering' from a condition.

The final thing I would like you to do is this. Do a quick internet search or look on your local newsagent's notice board or have a quick flick through the paper. Is there an advertisement for baby signing classes? Not singing, but *signing*. In recent years this has become quite a phenomenon. Yummy mummies are taking their little ones – babies who are well below the age we would expect them to be talking – to classes in local halls and leisure centres where they are taught the signs which will tell their mums that they want a drink, or they are tired, or a dozen other things. When people go to these classes, they tend to be amazed at what the babies pick up (and I'm talking about babies here, not toddlers). Grandparents are even more stunned. I'm not. All children have this capacity and some will prefer to communicate in this way as long as possible.

Put all of those things together and I would suggest that there has been a change in our outlook. The general perception of children has altered as we have become more focused on them, but this hasn't always worked to the benefit of the youngsters. Those whose intuition and psychic abilities are stronger than most are seen as plain odd. But why do we need to categorise them at all? Why can't we just revel in and celebrate whatever talents they possess? They are wise, can communicate, are caring and gifted. Does it really seem as if there is a problem?

Crystal children are especially kind and loving. They show enormous sensitivity and they are aware of people who are hurting spiritually. They also tend to look very striking, with huge, piercing eyes. Looking into their eyes is like looking into a deep pool of knowledge and ancient wisdom. They are mesmerising and, if you gaze at them, you may feel as if the child is looking deep inside you. For the uninitiated, this can be a chilling experience, but what you need to remember is that crystal children have no badness to them. They are just taking 'shortcuts'. While the rest of us adhere to social and cultural norms and expectations, crystal children walk their own path. They may stare into your eyes and maintain eye contact because they are reading you, and feel comfortable in doing so. They see no need to break this eye contact, because their wisdom allows them to get a lot out of the moment.

These children are intensely spiritual and very telepathic. Their gifts can make them likely to learn to talk later than their peers, challenging their parents' expectations about what they should have learned by which developmental stage. We need to let go of our rules and regulations, the little red books for babies, and the developmental milestones that it is all too easy for mums and dads (and other family members as well as teachers, doctors and carers in society) to worry about. Some seem so concerned about which boxes have been ticked that they don't actually recognise the individuality and marvellous ancient gifts a crystal child may possess.

Meeting crystal children

I can always spot crystal children because they have the most beautiful auras, with lots of pastel shades. I notice them and they notice me, because there is a recognition and sometimes a form of telepathic connection. As their name suggests, they are drawn to crystals and rock formations.

A number of years ago I was doing a show in Wales and began speaking to an older woman in the audience. Her mother was in the spirit world and I was able to confirm that she had passed over after a long struggle with pancreatic cancer. The mother was telling me about a small child aged about four, whose name was Felix. I felt this was a grandchild, and the woman confirmed this was correct. The mother told me that all this child did was hum along to music. He was as happy as Larry, but whenever he was doing anything it got his full attention – again, this was spot on.

I told her that Felix was a loving child who was always looking for cuddles and hugs and who had to be with people. I said that he had the most amazing eyes and it was as if he was looking right through you. He had only just started to speak, and his eyes communicated much more effectively than the words he spoke.

'That's amazing,' said the woman. 'I always say to my daughter that Felix can read your mind. She laughs at me, but his stare is so intense that I sometimes have to look away. I know that sounds mad but it's the only way I can describe it.'

I told her it wasn't mad at all. Felix was a crystal child and these were all examples of what crystal children do and the way they behave. He sounded typical.

There's a little boy in my extended family who is clearly a crystal child. He is happy, forgives easily, but had the typical developmental delay with speech. In fact, this little one, Greg, was four before he started to talk. He was always attracted to music and tone, while hating loud noises. These are typical traits of crystal children. They are here to help change the evolution of the planet, to make it a better place, and to follow the changes made by similar children before them, but strangely they have certain patterns of behaviour in common. Crystal children want to know what lies ahead, and Greg's interest was no different.

I hadn't seen Greg's mother, Wendy, for some years when I received a call from her one day, out of the blue. She tracked me down through a network of friends and contacts, and when she invited me to her house for a cup of tea I was happy to accept. As I have said before, I always feel there is a reason why people contact me, even if I'm not sure what that reason is at the start.

Greg was a lovely boy, and it was clear that he was Wendy's pride and joy, but she was concerned about him as well. 'I think that there might be a problem with Greg. Can you tell?'

I answered that, speaking as both a mum and a granny, he seemed like a wonderful child to me.

'No,' she said, 'that's not what I mean. Can you tell if he is – you know, all right? Is he all there?'

I raised my eyebrows, taken aback. While Greg hadn't spoken to me much, he had been friendly and warm. I was really drawn to his soul and energy. Of course, I suspected he was a crystal child from the moment I met him, but I was a little shocked that his own mother couldn't see that this boy was as far removed from 'problems' as it was possible to be.

'Wendy,' I said, 'let me ask you some things about Greg, then I'll tell you, without a shadow of a doubt, whether he's "all there".' She looked relieved and I asked her just what I will ask you now. If you have any of the suspicions Wendy had, apply these questions to your own child.

- Do they have beautiful, deep, large eyes?
- Are they very sensitive?
- Do they always seem to know what you need and whether you are sad or lost?
- Did they start talking much later than their friends?
- Was this 'inability' no problem for them because they could always make you understand what they wanted?
- Did they sometimes make you feel they could read your mind?
- Have they always been a fussy eater? Many crystal children are vegetarian from an early age as they cannot bear the thought of other creatures being abused.
- Are they very intelligent?
- Have other people told you that there is a 'problem' with your child?
- Do they forgive people very easily and trust everyone? Look out for the way they will hand over their toys to

anyone who asks for them, no matter how they are treated by them.

- Have there been times when they seem to see things that are invisible to you?
- Are they drawn to things to do with belief and the supernatural?

Wendy was shaking by the time I had asked her these questions.

'I can't believe you haven't been around him the whole time since the day he was born,' she said. 'It's as if you've known him forever.'

'I have!' I laughed. 'Children like Greg are old souls and he is exactly the sort of person who makes me feel as if we have known each other since the dawn of time.'

I explained to her about crystal children and their amazing talents, and urged her not to think of her wonderful boy as a 'problem' but as a gift. The parents of crystal children are blessed. They have been chosen for a reason and their child is with them for a reason. Crystal children are here to learn and here to teach; anyone who comes in contact with them should bear that in mind for their own time on this plane as well.

An angel on earth

I was once invited to do a reading for a woman named Glenda. She was different to Wendy in that she was full of joy about her son from the moment I walked in the door. The boy was with her when I arrived.

'This is Jay,' she told me, introducing him. 'He's my angel on earth.'

How lovely to hear a mother talk about her child that way! Jay, who was nine years old, had many of the characteristics of crystal children and according to Glenda he was a very gifted boy. He was a very verbal child, and had been since he was young, which shows that there is flexibility within any schema, but also that crystal children will be what they want to be.

We needed privacy for the reading, but it wasn't Glenda who suggested this; it was Jay. 'I'm going upstairs now, Mum,' he said, 'so that you can talk to the lady.' He gave me a warm hug and smiled, then left. Of course, I knew that he wouldn't have to be in the room with us to know what was going on because he was so highly intuitive.

I swear Glenda would have spent the whole session talking about Jay! He was the apple of her eye, and I could see why. 'He is such a gifted child,' she said. 'It's as if he knows about things before he even tries them.'

'Has that always been the case?' I asked.

'Oh, without a doubt,' she replied. 'His dad has gone so it's only him and me, but I never feel lonely.'

'I can sense that when your husband left it was Jay who gave you advice, wasn't it?'

'How could you know that?' she asked. 'He was only four at the time!'

I come across some instances in which people are far too keen to tell children all of their worries and woes. They burden the poor wee things and expect them to grow up far too soon, but that wasn't the case here. That isn't what happens with crystal children. Jay would have known about his mother's pain even though she told me that she and her estranged husband never argued in front of the boy. In fact, the problem in the relationship was that her ex was emotionally frozen, so there weren't any arguments, just silences. Jay became his mother's guide without her asking him to take on that role, simply because he knew everything that was going on and because he was so in tune with Glenda. He was in tune with his father too, as his sensitivity didn't exclude anyone.

'I used to be amazed at what he came out with,' confided Glenda, 'but also a bit ashamed that my four-year-old had more sense and a better handle on the situation than I ever had. He told me that his dad was "limiting" me. He makes many comments that are way beyond his years.'

That's because crystal children *are* way beyond their years! I asked Glenda if she had always felt that Jay was the parent in their relationship, and she became very emotional.

'Yes, I do,' she said, 'and I feel so bad about that. He's only a little boy and yet he takes so much on.'

'I bet he never seems to carry a heavy load, though,' I pointed out. 'I bet that he is always sensitive but also content in what he knows. You will be no burden to him. He loves you dearly and he is a child who is here to love and to learn.'

I told Glenda that Jay was a crystal child and explained about their characteristics. On top of that, I was able to connect with spirit to get some evidence of their daily relationship, all of which helped to prove to Glenda that her son was part of this amazing breed and that I was speaking from experience.

I was able to tell Glenda that there would be much more of this type of interaction as Jay got older, and that his own psychic abilities would increase. I also explained to her that Jay would probably start talking about his past lives, if he hadn't already done so, and that she shouldn't freak out about it. It can be a strange experience for the parents and loved ones of crystal children to be faced with a barrage of stories about their past lives almost as soon as they open their mouths. The thing to remember is that, although your child may not have been verbal for long before these recollections begin, they will have been trying to tell you for a long time. They will be so used to the experiences they can recall that it will not seem odd to them. It is only odd to those who decide to categorise it that way.

If you are one of the lucky ones who is the parent of one of these wonderful souls, you may find that you have to be completely reconditioned. That is one of the gifts they will bring you. All the restrictions and rules you place on yourself will seem less important once you awaken to the beauty of the crystal child's world. Your son or daughter may be connected to and speaking with angels – are you ready for that? If not, why not? What do you have to lose? Actually, you have a *lot* to lose if you remain closed. All psychic children have so much to teach us that we would be fools if we didn't listen and learn.

They just know

I once went to do a reading for a woman who couldn't get a babysitter for her three-year-old son. She asked whether it would be all right if he stayed beside us and I said that was okay. As long as we got the time for the reading, I didn't mind at all. I asked whether he needed a lot of attention, but she insisted that he was always happy just playing on his own.

When I arrived at the house, this wee boy was sitting on the carpet drawing and singing away to himself. As I came into the room, he stopped what he was doing and stared at me intensely as if he were sussing me out. I held his gaze until he seemed to have had enough and went back to his drawing. As I sat down with his mother I said, 'He's been here a few times, hasn't he?'

'That's what everyone says,' she laughed. 'He's like a wee man cut short. He just seems to know what's happening all the time.'

I told her about crystal children and their traits – she'd never heard of them before – and I also told her that his gran, who was in spirit, had been very psychic. She agreed with this and I went on to tell her that there had been a connection in their family for years. There was no need to worry about this child, because he was very content. He was like a security guard for the house, she said, because he always checked everyone out. What a great soul he had!

My own grandson, Colin, is another example of a crystal child. It took him a long time to start speaking and we could all see that he was very frustrated by it. Both he and my granddaughter Ellie are blessed to have such a special mum in my daughter Dannielle, because her own talents mean that she understands them completely.

Colin has large eyes, he loves cuddles, and he would listen to music all day and all night. He is very well connected to all types of energy. He instinctively knows how people feel and often comes out with things that lift their spirits. Music in particular helped him enormously when he was at the non-verbal stage. Colin would always be humming or dancing, and this seemed to be a release for him; however, he hated music to be loud and always covered his ears if it was, because he was very sensitive in a sensory capacity as well as a psychic one.

Colin comes out with the most amazing comments. One evening, when he was eight, we were all watching television when there was an advert with a black man in it. Colin turned to his mum and asked, 'Is that Al Jolson?' Now, I can hardly remember him and I'm a good fifty years older than wee Colin, so I wonder where that comment came from? He didn't seem to know anything about Al Jolson when we asked. I'm certain that it was simply a spontaneous remark from a past life.

Colin is a very emotional little boy and gets terribly upset if someone else has been hurt or offended. He likes to offer reassurance that everything will be fine. All crystal children are incredibly loving; if only we could all be like that.

When Colin was much younger, he used to speak about a woman in his room. 'She walks from my room to the bathroom,' he told me. Crystal children can and do pick up on the presence of the other side, and depending on how they are in themselves they can either deal with it or not. Colin is not very comfortable and would prefer it wasn't there. Personally I feel that as he gets a little older this aspect of his talent will settle more, but, if it doesn't, then he can do what his mum did when she was younger and choose to block it out until such time as he feels it is right to have it in his life.

Once you realise that you are host to a crystal child you will find life much easier, because crystal children need less parenting. They keep themselves busy and they are highly intelligent. They love to feel their connection to Mother Earth and if you can encourage and facilitate this, so much the better. They will adore being outdoors, and they will enjoy being around animals, going for woodland walks, sensing the natural energy around them – it almost tops them up. They will have a million questions for you, and you will not know all of the answers, so learn with them, because they will respect you more if you accept that all of life, on this plane and the next, is a learning process.

Above all, be thankful. All children are an incredible gift, but with your crystal child by your side life will be an adventure. You are one of the lucky ones.

Chapter 9

The wonder all around us

We are all surrounded by magnetic energy fields, known as auras, and psychics and mediums can tap into this energy for information relating to people, situations and events in their lives. When I work with someone, I link into their aura and it's as if they were a book. All I have to do is take them off the shelf and open the pages to have a good read. Another way to think of it is that it's as if my invisible arm reaches out, retrieves the information from the person and brings it back for me. There are many ways to work with intuition, and some are startling, but they have never failed me yet.

There are some other 'professions' in which similar approaches to energy are used. A very good friend of mine called Jean is a physiotherapist and healer. She has worked with many clients over the years, and one story she told me in particular struck a chord. She was approached by a woman who wanted her to work with her son, a young boy called Alex, who was hyperactive. His mum wanted Jean to see if she could calm him down – those were her words. Now, that phrase alone set Jean's radar off, because it told her more about the person saying it than the young boy it was applied to.

'What exactly is it you want me to do?' asked Jean.

'He's just not up for sitting still, he can't be doing with it. I'd like you to make him calmer.'

Jean thought about this for a moment, then said, 'First of all, would you mind if I did some work with you?'

'Me?' asked the boy's mother. 'It's him I want sorted!'

'Don't worry, I won't charge,' said Jean, and the woman agreed.

Jean started to work on her in a healing sense, calming her aura rather than her son's. All the time she kept an eye on the boy, who had indeed been very fretful and active since he arrived. Within a few minutes of the healing work beginning, Alex changed. He calmed down. He relaxed. Jean found his reaction much more interesting than that of his mother. After a while, he moved over to his mum's side and held her hand.

'He's never done that before of his own free will,' she whispered.

Jean suggested that she just keep quiet and take her cues from Alex. 'Let him be, and he'll settle if he wants to.'

Jean worked on the woman for almost an hour, balancing her chakras and doing general healing work. Both the woman and Alex remained silent throughout, and he was completely calm. This was a lovely example of the invisible energy bond that exists between mother and child. By simply working on the woman, a connection was made with the child's energy, things just happened and she found the calmer side to her son that she had been trying to force, unsuccessfully, for years. Those precious moments together changed their relationship for ever.

I am not saying that there is no bond between a biological father and his child, or none between a woman and a baby that is not biologically hers, but I do believe that there is an even stronger bond where the mother has carried a baby for nine months and nurtured it throughout the pregnancy. Conception and birth are beautiful miracles, which many people take for granted. If you stop for a moment and think about how life is made, it almost beggars belief. Is it therefore any surprise that the resulting relationship between mother and child is also incredible?

Gillian and her children

I once visited a woman called Gillian who had six children – a very large family by today's standards. She was a complete earth mother, who adored every one of her brood equally and revelled in her status as a mum. As you can imagine, she had a lot to juggle in her life and it had to run with almost military precision. The reason she had asked me to read for her was that she and her husband were planning to move house and she wanted to know if it was the right decision. It would be a huge upheaval for all of the children and she wanted to know if it would be worth it. Money was tight (unsurprisingly!) and the couple couldn't afford to move again if they found they didn't like the new house.

As soon as the reading began, I told her that I could see she had been very drawn to one particular property but she was worried that it would be a financial stretch, so she was now considering another house and doubting her own judgement.

'You think that first house would be perfect, don't you? But you are getting down about the money side of things. You feel that your dream home is slipping away but that you shouldn't fight for it because it would mean the purse strings were tight in the beginning.'

'It's as if you've been listening in on my discussions with my husband!' she said – a comment I hear quite a lot. 'That's just how I feel. I'm stuck between a rock and a hard place.'

Actually, to my mind, she wasn't. I felt that her dream house *was* within her reach and her only fear was one that could be overcome. Gillian was worried that there would be no additional cash for the children. If they needed any extras, the family would be left short.

'Yes, you're right, that's absolutely it. I hate to think that I might not be able to give them what they need.'

Gillian didn't seem to see that she was a brilliant mum and that she already provided well for her children, both emotionally and materially. I had something to tell her that might put things in perspective. 'Two of your younger children have already picked up on this vibe,' I informed her. 'They have been talking about it all.'

'I don't know how they could know,' she said. 'We never discuss things like that with them. We like to keep all the worry away from them.'

'Children don't need to be told. If there's a strong link between you, they'll pick up on it, and that's what's happening. They're not talking about words, they're talking about your feelings. They know what you've been thinking.'

Gillian was really shocked, and paused as if struck dumb, then agreed with me. 'They *have* said something, actually. You're quite right. Only the other evening one of my youngest boys, Jack, was sitting beside me and, out of nowhere, he said that if they ever needed anything I always managed to get it for them. Then his sister Kiera, who is a year older, said that we should move. I thought both comments came out of nowhere and weren't even connected with each other. Are you saying they've been listening in to my worries as I run them through in my head?'

I told her that was exactly what had been happening and that she should be very proud of the psychic abilities of her children. She clearly had a wonderful bond with them, which was based on love and nurturing, and they were showing her just how strong it was by allowing her to realise that they were often inside her head. The bond between Gillian and all of her children was tight, but these two in particular always seemed to come out with particularly apposite comments. Sometimes it takes a complete stranger to point things out before they become visible. I told her that the kids were right – she *did* always do the right thing by them, and this move would be no different. The house she wanted was the dream home for all of them, not just some notion of hers alone, and by moving there she would be giving them so much. I knew things would work out for the best.

The gift of intuition

I get approached by many women who are at a turning point in their lives. Sometimes they are ending a relation-ship (or wondering if they should), and sometimes they are thinking about a family move, as Gillian was. Heather came to me because she had just separated from her part-ner. Even before she revealed the break-up, I could see that things had been tough for her over the past two years and that she felt very alone. I saw that her partner had left very suddenly and it was all a bit of a shock to her. It was only after he left that she found out that he had been cheating on her for years and that he had gone off to be with his new woman. All of this was spot on.

'You've been very protective of your daughter since the split, haven't you?' I asked, and she nodded. 'But I'm seeing that there has always been a deep bond between the two of you.' Actually, *bond* did not fully describe what I meant. These two had more of a *knowing* when things weren't right for the other.

'I've definitely always felt that way about her; since long before she could talk, I've known if she was just a bit off,' said Heather, 'but I only found out recently that it cuts both ways and she can work out how I am without me saying a word.'

Heather's daughter, Alanna, was now seven and very sensitive and intuitive. I could see that, after the separation, the wee girl went through a bad time at school as she was picked on a lot. Heather kept listening to what I had to say, but she was getting emotional.

'You had a strong feeling that something was wrong. It just kept niggling at you, isn't that right?' I could see a very clear image in my mind, which I relayed to Heather. One day, just as she and Alanna were heading out, Heather asked, out of the blue, 'What's wrong at school?'

Heather took up the story by saying that Alanna gave a big sigh when she asked, and told her all about it. 'Alanna had never looked as if there was something wrong. I just had a really strong vibe, as if something or someone was pushing me to ask the question. I don't know where it came from. I've always felt close to her, but I've never felt that shove before. It was almost physical.'

Just before the split, while Alanna and her mum were playing a game, the wee girl said to her, 'What will it be like when we are on our own?' Heather had brushed the comment off, thinking it was a throwaway remark as there had been no indication that the relationship was going to flounder, and she never pursued it, but when her partner left, Alanna's words came back to her loud and clear.

The invisible bond cannot be denied and there are hundreds of stories about mothers calling their children just before or after something has happened – just knowing something was wrong without any clue why. If you are a mother reading this, I am sure that you will have at one point experienced this yourself. I would urge everyone to develop this gift to its fullest potential as it is incredibly useful, even for the cynics amongst us. Surely we all need as much protection as we can get? Developing your intuition should be a skill that is a natural part of your tool kit. When sharpened, it can be an internal compass that leads you in the correct direction every time. Life doesn't come with a guarantee, but if you work on your intuitive skills you will get as close to that as possible.

Intuition is simply the art of knowing by attuning yourself to your inner senses. Guidance exists naturally within you and is one of your most valued gifts. It's interesting to see how many people run around chasing their tails, looking for information outside of themselves, when in fact the very thing they seek is in there, inside them, all the time. We rarely give ourselves credit for knowing which way to go, where the journey will take us or indeed how our lives will shape up. It's little wonder that we are in crisis mode most of the time. By taking ten minutes now and again to sit and allow the information we need to surface, we will find that we are provided with amazing insight and are saved from endless hours of worry and futile running or searching. We can learn so much from psychic children who just *know* in such a natural way. They are totally in tune with the core of their own being, and we adults should follow their lead.

It staggers me that so many people deny what is a part of them. You wouldn't ignore what your eyes saw, or think that what you were hearing was a figment of the imagination, but the sixth sense is often ridiculed and mocked. The last laugh is on those who do not tap into the power that lies within. Crystal children lead the way, and they are more powerful as a result.

Why do we resist developing what is our own? Why do we create chaos, when we could have answers? Why do we make it difficult for ourselves? It really doesn't need to be this way. Nobody can say that they do not have, or have never experienced, intuition. It is there every day of our lives in hundreds of different ways. It tells us that we should call home, diverts us from danger and stops us heading down a blind alley. It puts us in the right place at the right time, warns us off certain people and sends out flashes when we are making the wrong choices.

If you look back over certain events in your life, I am sure that there were points when you *knew* there was something not quite right in the whole scheme of things. However, I bet you didn't always listen, did you? You would dismiss it as '*just a feeling*', as if feelings didn't matter!

Why do we persist in repeating old patterns? Maybe we feel that things need to be difficult in order to get something from them. I would urge you to smash that way of thinking right now. Nothing needs to be difficult unless you make it so, and it is within your control to make changes which will allow your intuition to give you whatever you need. Set it a task as a test and see what comes up. Maybe you will be pleasantly surprised. What do you have to lose?

I would also suggest that you encourage your children to develop their intuition as, with your support, they can learn to embrace this side of their being at a much earlier age if they see and feel your acceptance of it. There are lots of fun ways you can do this, but let me tell you one of my favourites. You'll need lots of old birthday or Christmas cards (you'll never throw old cards away again once you discover this game). Take three or four cards from the pile at random, and make sure that your child doesn't know who they are from – Christmas cards may be better when they are young, as they tend to remember every single birthday card sender and the picture on them all; similarly, make sure you don't choose the ones which say anything like, *To a Special Grandson*, as that will give the game away!

Ask your child to look at each card and see if they can tell you as much as possible about who they think sent it. Ask the following questions:

- Are they male or female?
- Are they an adult or a child, old or young?
- What does the person looks like?
- Where do they live?
- What type of car do they drive?
- Do they have any pets?
- Do they have any funny habits?
- Do they have any noticeable physical characteristics?

You could add your own questions to this list. The more information the child provides you with, the better. They should get a point for each piece of correct information.

I would suggest that you keep a little notebook because you will be amazed at how their talent develops and you may not believe it unless it is written down.

It would also be interesting to see if the child's 'performance', for want of a better word, differs when their mum is involved, as opposed to their dad, or if someone outside their immediate family plays instead of a sibling. I would also suggest that you see whether your child picks up more about one branch of the family tree, as this may be where their psychic connection lies.

I have suggested this game, and others like it, to lots of people and they are always amazed at what happens. I'm not, because I know children are psychic, but I'm still tickled by it.

I know full well that the bond between mother and child is one which survives passing over. Make the most of your time on this plane by playing lots of games (there are more in chapter 16), and having lots of fun, but rest assured that the link will not be broken when one of you passes over.

Letting the cat out of the bag

Very recently, I was doing a reading for a woman called Gail. The first communication I received was actually from Gail's father-in-law, who began by showing me a bandstand in a public park, which was clearly very significant. Gail had played a lot at this bandstand as a child and had always felt drawn to it. I could tell from the images and feelings I was being sent that she had been a potentially psychic child but it had never been noticed or encouraged; however, this bandstand had been an important place during her childhood. She always felt a pull towards it and didn't understand why.

One day, she went there in the rain to meet some friends. Despite it pouring down, Gail just knew she had to go there, but the weather was so bad that she suspected no one else would turn up. When she arrived, she was met by a shocking sight – a local homeless man had hanged himself from the roof. What was amazing was that Gail wasn't unduly upset by this at all, and I think this was a reflection of her own childhood intuition. She continued to visit the bandstand for years, and when I mentioned the story to her, although she was surprised that I knew, she still took it in her stride.

I then moved on to talk to her mother. She wasn't alone; Gail's dad had moved to her side while I talked with her, and Gail's maternal uncle, a very happy soul, was also with her. I told Gail that I could see a man holding a crystal ball and laughing a lot.

'Yes, that sounds like Uncle Ray,' she said.

'Your mum doesn't look amused, though – I can tell that they are very different characters. She thinks this is all nonsense, doesn't she?'

'She did,' confirmed Gail. 'But how can she think that now?'

'She isn't a woman who bothers about contradictions!' I told her. 'Despite the fact that she's there, giving out information from the other side, she's still a bit of a cynic.' I had to laugh at that! Gail told me that her mother had never been 'into this type of thing', whereas her uncle was a frequent visitor to mediums and psychic shows. I found it fascinating that they had been so opposite to each other in their beliefs on this plane, and yet were together, both communicating from the other side.

Gail had two young children, a girl and a boy, and I could tell that the first born was very psychic – unsurprising, given their mum's talents. Both Arlene and JJ were very connected, but it was JJ who really drew me in.

'He sees things, doesn't he?'

Gail nodded, and smiled.

'He's always been that way,' I continued, 'and he is very interested in spirit matters, but not sure how to handle it all.'

Gail agreed. 'He's very young.'

Yes, he was only four, but I told Gail that she shouldn't really think of JJ in terms of how many birthdays he had celebrated on this plane because he was a little boy who had been here before. He was unsure of how to deal with things, but he wasn't scared. 'He sees his grandfather, doesn't he?' I asked.

'Yes, he does – but there's something there that he can't work out. He says that my dad carries something with him, but he isn't sure what. Can you have a chat with my son?'

I was delighted to meet JJ. Often parents tell me about their psychic children, but I never ask directly to meet them or pry into what they are capable of, for many reasons. As I've said, I don't normally give readings for children under the age of eighteen, as they could be left feeling confused. However, the fact that JJ and Arlene had such a supportive mum, and that she had been through similar experiences as a child herself, made me feel that there would be understanding in their life, and that their mum would not panic or be negative about their wonderful gifts. Respect for the child is also very important to me – they are psychic, just as I am, so in some ways I'm actually dealing with someone who is more like me than many other adults.

JJ came in, and I was very impressed by the way Gail spoke to him. She told him that I was a friend who sometimes talks to people who aren't here any longer and that I was really interested in how he could see his granddad.

'Is that right, JJ?' I asked. 'You can see things too?'

He nodded and said, 'All the time.'

'Isn't that lucky?' I remarked.

JJ looked at his mum and asked, 'Why is it lucky?'

'Well,' I went on, 'there are some lovely folk watching over you – you've already seen your granddad, and there are more. They all love you so much and it is very special that you can still have this connection with them.'

'Can I ask you something?' the little boy said. 'When I see my granddad, he's got something with him, but I don't know what it is. It's like a big purple bag, but I think I'm meant to know what it means. There's something else too – it's black and white, but it won't stay still long enough for me to know what it is. Sometimes, when I see Granddad, Millie walks past and it all gets even fuzzier.' Millie was their Siamese cat, and this was just the clue I needed to match up all the pieces for this lovely child.

'When Millie is there,' I asked, 'do you see things more easily, even if you can't see inside the purple bag and the black and white thing is fuzzy?'

'Yes, yes I do. Granddad is clearer and I can see trees and things, but ...'

'The fuzzy thing? Yes, I know! I bet you're really cross that you can't work out what that is, aren't you?' I smiled at JJ, who giggled right back. 'Well, you can blame Millie for the good things and the things which make you cross,' I informed the little lad.

In fact, what JJ was experiencing was auric energy. Millie was channelling some of this too and the boy was so sensitive and intuitive that he was getting mixed messages. His grandfather was coming through more clearly, but the 'fuzzy thing' was becoming less distinct.

'I bet you had a cat when you were little, didn't you?' I asked Gail. 'A black and white one? I bet your dad was very fond of that cat too.'

'Pooky!' Gail exclaimed.

'That's what JJ is seeing – your own cat is fuzzying up the energy of the cat who is with your father. You know, JJ, you're a very special little boy. Do you know what I think you should do? The next time you see your grand-dad, you should just ask him what he has brought with him. Ask him what's in the purple bag. He'll be able to show you Pooky much more clearly and I bet he will help you lots with your talent.'

JJ was a very gifted child, and I'm really looking forward to catching up with him again and watching how he develops. There is a wonder in psychic children; they bring immeasurable beauty to our lives. You may have such children in your life and your family – if so, you are as blessed as they are, and I hope that you will cherish the connections which can be made.

Chapter 10

Indigo children

Indigo children can become crystal children if their gifts are nurtured and they continue to progress with their skills. They have been with us for over a hundred years and they are here for nothing less than to change the planet. Indigos are souls with great wisdom about them. They don't like to conform to the needs of society and often rebel against everything. This makes them mavericks in their own way, but their intuitive and psychic skills are also very highly attuned.

My nine-year-old granddaughter Ellie is one of these souls. From birth, she has astounded us with her gift and the beauty of her capabilities. To Ellie, it is all so natural, and that in itself is wonderful to watch. She is very psychic and comes out with information that is astounding. Every so often she will say, 'Right, Gran, get the cards out,' and will give me a Tarot reading. She often gives me amazingly accurate details about clients, despite the fact that I never discuss my work with anyone in my family – all of the stories in this book will be news to them.

One day, some years ago, Ellie predicted that I would work with a particular man, who had been mentioned to me in the course of a reading with someone else, but whom I didn't know personally. Not only did Ellie say that I would be working in a professional capacity with him in the near future, but she also described him so accurately that I was shocked when I met him for the first time.

Ellie doesn't see anything unusual in what she can do, which is one of the noticeable traits of indigo children. Indigos test limits in their own way, by asking pertinent questions and challenging their elders, and it all seems very logical *to them* that they would do these things, even though it can blow others away.

Standing up to bullies

When I went to see a woman called Eileen, she told me a story about her daughter. Eileen was under great pressure at work from a woman who was bullying her. She had been depressed about it and unsure what to do, bound up as she was in office politics and adult worries about 'telling'. One night, while she was sitting watching TV with her daughter, the little girl – Marie – made a comment out of the blue: 'You know, Mummy, if you don't stand up for yourself, the same thing will keep happening.'

Eileen looked at her daughter in shock. It wasn't the first time that the ten-year-old girl had come out with something so relevant to her mother's life, even though Eileen always made sure that she didn't burden her child with any of her own worries. 'What do you mean?' she asked.

'Well, I saw this woman in my dreams and she was being really horrible to you. I know that it is happening at your work. She's very bad. I wanted to tell her that she shouldn't do these things to you. Why don't you stand up to her?' Marie asked.

'How do you know that I don't?' Eileen countered, trying to laugh it off.

Marie was very serious as she looked at her mother. She took her hand and looked deep into her eyes. 'Mum, I know about it because I saw it. You don't stand up to her, you just take it. You were standing there, not saying anything, not doing anything. You have to stand up for yourself,' she repeated. 'If you don't, she'll never stop and, even if you leave, you'll never forgive yourself for taking it from her.'

Marie went back to watching TV and eating snacks as if this was all perfectly natural – which, to me, it is! She said nothing else that evening, but Eileen couldn't get her wise daughter's words out of her mind. By the end of the evening, she had determined it was a sign. The next day, at work, she stopped the woman in mid-flow as she began one of her verbal attacks.

'This is the last time you will treat me like this,' Eileen said. 'It will stop, and it will stop now.'

The woman backed down straight away and it never happened again. Eileen was in a much better place because of her child's sixth sense and ability to help her put the message across in a simple but effective way. From what she told me – this and a few other stories – I was sure that Marie was an indigo child. She wasn't doing very well at school – not through any lack of intelligence, but because she was incredibly bored. Some indigos are disruptive because of the lack of stimulation they are given. They start to fidget and what they do can seem to teachers like 'playing up'. It's not the teachers who are at fault, though – the needs of indigo children ought to be included as part of teacher training.

Indigos are not helped by being pushed into behavioural boxes, as they are deep and profound individuals. I've previously noted the ways in which they're often 'diagnosed' (I hate that word) and given labels of ADHD or ADD; yet these children don't need drugs or treatment – they are special souls, and their gifts are often completely overlooked. How sad. There is a big difference between bad behaviour and psychic skills. And for as long as our society remains one which can't be bothered to look that wee bit deeper into who people really are, the same type of 'problem' is likely to recur.

If you are a parent or a teacher, a doctor or a social worker, a grandparent or a police officer, I would love for you to do a little bit of research into the phenomenon of indigo children because by arming yourself with that knowledge you could actually change the way you view things and perhaps even make your job or role a whole lot easier. Ask yourself these questions about the children you deal with:

- Does the child have a strong sense of who they are and act very surprised when others don't recognise the person they are?
- Does the child act as if they are almost royalty and that they don't have to adhere to the same rules as everyone else? (Don't dismiss this as narcissism; open your mind to the other possibilities.)
- Do they tend to tell adults what to do, without rudeness or cheek, just because they know?
- Do they find it difficult to do simple but restrictive things such as standing in queues or waiting for their turn? (They simply don't see the point!)
- Do they get frustrated by boring tasks and repetition, but flower when directed creatively – and lose sense of time when they are doing the latter?
- Do they always see a better way of doing things and are they very vocal in pointing this out?
- Do they refuse to accept absolute authority for its own sake, and react against phrases such as 'Because I said so,' or 'Respect your elders'? (This is because they see no value in being told something just 'is'.)

- Do they seem antisocial and excluded, especially at school? This will change if they socialise with other indigos.

Life isn't always easy for indigo children. They have come to Earth to do a major thing – change everything, change everyone – and they are largely misunderstood. They are like time travellers. They have come from every part of the spirit world for their purpose here, but rather than welcome and help them we constantly put obstacles in their way. They are pushing against the grain, battling into the wind, and they need tremendous strength to keep doing so. Not only do they have no interest in or recognition of many rules and regulations, but they also don't have the time to abide by them when they are tuned in to a higher reckoning.

I'm far from being an authority on indigo (or crystal) children, but I do recognise their talents and the misunderstanding they face, because that is what so many people with spiritual connections have to deal with. So much of what I have read about these children chimes with what I felt as a little girl myself; I always felt different – or strange – and that, although I didn't fit in, I still had a reason to be here. I still feel that way, actually; the only difference now is that I don't mind – I understand that it is part of who I am.

A child called Sally

Indigo children are extraordinarily psychically gifted. Some of their gifts are at what we might consider to be the extreme end of the spectrum, including those who are skilled at telepathy and telekinesis (the power to move objects with the mind). Indigo children help advance evolution in many ways, by starting projects that encourage peace on earth and gathering others to assist them. We will never know how many of the great inventions and developments of our civilisation in the last hundred years have been made by indigos.

One evening, I was reading cards for a lady called Gemma. I could see that she was a terrible worrier, even over things that didn't really matter. Her partner, on the other hand, was the total opposite. However, it was her two daughters who had the real story that interested me. One of them, Ava, was very laid back and easygoing, just like her dad, but the other daughter, Sally, was a real challenge. This girl didn't just challenge her family, she challenged her teachers and everyone else around her too. Now, from what you have read so far in this chapter you probably suspect that Sally was an indigo child, and you'd be absolutely right. I told Gemma that Sally was a little girl with lots of her own opinions and that she would not shift from them.

'She's a right little madam,' Gemma said.

I could see how some people might describe Sally that way, but they would be doing her a remarkable disservice.

'There's no talking to her sometimes,' Gemma went on. 'And the school is finding it very hard to work out what to do with her.'

I was shocked; the school didn't have to *do* anything with her at all apart from let her be herself and keep her stimulated.

'I am a bit worried,' said Gemma. 'She's only seven and she's like this already – I think there will be tough times ahead and things will only get worse. What should I do?'

I told Gemma that, yes, Sally was challenging the system, but that was what she was put on Earth for. 'She is a sensitive child who has a strong sense of what is right and wrong. I know that she comes out with the most amazing things and remarkable pieces of information. You're speechless sometimes, aren't you?'

'Absolutely! You've described her perfectly, but I still don't know what to do.'

'If people could just understand that Sally's boredom threshold is limited and that she needs to be mentally stretched then this would make such a difference. Your daughter is dealing with amazing things. She is developing her psychic skills, receiving miraculous communications, and thinking she can change the world – while all around her people are only thinking of how they can make her conform in order to make their own lives easier. Well, do you know what? It will only make their lives easier in the short run, because your daughter will be able to do amazing things only if she is allowed to spread her wings.'

'That's just how I feel,' said Gemma, 'but all I hear is that people want her to sort herself out, to stop making waves and to settle into things. She's only seven years old! I've tried to tell them, I've tried to tell school, but it all falls on deaf ears.'

Sadly, Gemma was right. What she was describing can often be the case, as indigos are here to challenge the system and shake us all up a bit. They are not supposed to be easygoing children; it is their role in society to help push for change, and this was the case with Sally. In a few years, I hope to discover that her mum was strong enough to make her the person she needed to be – and that the rest of the world allowed this to happen.

How to help an indigo

There are many things you can do to help your own indigos. You must bear in mind that indigos are trailblazers and they have a deep desire to lead the way; they need to be stimulated and they enjoy anything which makes them think or which challenges them. If you want to help them and grow their intuition at the same time, then you need to come up with some interesting games.

If your child is under seven, try this game; every time the phone rings at home, answer it, and then ask them to guess who it is. It would be best to keep a notepad by the side of the phone so that you can take notes and tot up scores over a week or a month. To make it a bit more interesting, you need to speak to your indigo in their own language. Tell them that if they know the person who is on the phone, that's great – but if the caller is a stranger to them or if they don't know their name, then they should go on their feelings or the 'pictures' in their head. They could try and think of a Disney or fairytale character who they feel would 'fit' the person.

So, for example, let's say that the child tells you that they are seeing the Fairy Godmother from *Sleeping Beauty*. This implies someone who is female, older and good-natured; someone who the child feels has a touch of magic about them and around whom they feel comfortable. Do you see what I mean?

Let's try another example. If the child came up with Pinocchio, that could refer to someone young, but it's more likely to be a comment on their immaturity. We all know that the little wooden boy told lies, so think about what it is in the person who is calling that they might be picking up on, and why?

Similarly, they won't say Goldilocks because they think the caller knows three bears. They will use that name because the person maybe has a tendency to take what isn't hers, or to go where she hasn't been invited, or to never be satisfied with things (although she will be likely to have blonde hair, be pretty and have a very persuasive manner). They won't say Buzz Lightyear because your boss who is calling to ask you to work overtime actually thinks he's a Space Ranger, but he might very well be the sort of person who doesn't recognise the reality of situations or who thinks he can always resolve situations (rescue people) when it is actually everyone around him doing the hard work. However, he will be likely to appear physically strong and be a very likeable, kind individual.

When playing the game, remember to remain open-minded and continue to think on the child's wavelength; then you will both get so much more out of it. It is a fun game for the child and probably quite easy for them to do, but at the same time it allows them to show you their skills, and that is important for them. Your indigo – or crystal, or any psychic child – will love the fact that you are interested and will relish the opportunity to show you what they can do.

If your child is over seven years of age, then they are most likely to tell you what they can sense, see and feel, so why not get them to write a little story and draw a picture of who they think may have been on the phone? Look at the words and the colours they use as they are all indicators of what they are really sensing. Colours can relate to feelings and emotions as well.

Sometimes indigo children have elements of a truly amazing condition called synaesthesia. The Synaesthesia Association describes this as 'a union of the senses' whereby two or more of the five senses (or six, as I believe we all have) that are normally experienced separately become joined together. Some children who have this will experience colour when they read words. They may taste sounds. They may smell shapes. This is all automatic for them and they can't turn it on or off. It isn't harmful at all – in fact, it's rather wonderful for most. Your indigo may have partial or complete synaesthesia, so bear this in mind when they try to describe anything to you, and in particular when playing this game.

What indigos can tell us

The wonder of these talented individuals is never-ending. Ellie, my granddaughter, is the one who has really opened my eyes to the abilities of indigos and I bless her for it. One day I was sitting in the car with her. I can't actually recall why – maybe we were waiting for someone. She was about five years old at the time. I put out my hand to her, as I often did, not because she is a palmist but it was just something which I had started to do quite recently. I would say, 'Come on, Ellie – what do you see?'

That day she took my hand and looked at it intently. She wasn't looking at the rings on my fingers or anything like that; she was just staring as she always did – and does – when she is in psychic mode. She told me some things that were relevant to my life and I loved the fact that she could do all of this. Then, all of a sudden, she closed my hand, pushed it back towards me, and said, 'Gran, that's all I can tell you. It's not my place to tell you about your life – it's yours to find out.' You could have knocked me down with a feather – she was five years old! They were such prophetic words from a little child, but this is how indigos work. They just come out with things that are intense and real. They are a miracle.

With Ellie, the whole palm-reading thing had started off as a bit of fun when she was a toddler, but she took to it very quickly. Once, she'd held my hand very quickly and said, 'Auntie Rita's coming over next week.' I dismissed her words as Rita lived in Ireland at the time and there was no reason for her to visit unannounced. But Ellie insisted. 'You're wrong,' she said. 'She'll be here.' Sure enough, within days I got a call from Rita to say that, she didn't know why, but she had an awful urge to come over for a visit – and so she did.

On another occasion, when Ellie was giving me one of her famous readings, she said that my work would be growing and that I would be moving to a very quiet place with trees all around. In terms of the work issue, she was very specific. She told me that I would meet a man through a business appointment who would do a lot for me professionally. She spoke as a mature adult, not a child who had barely started school. 'Your cards are all running in sequence,' she told me, 'and I see that this man will offer you an opportunity which could be really big. He's a bit full of himself and likes the women, so watch yourself.'

I found this last comment really funny, but promised Ellie that I certainly would watch out for such a man. As it happened, although she didn't know it, I had met a man who I'd sensed would do something very important for me. He was exactly as she described and we were going to meet and see if we could take things further. It turned out that I did some work with his son who was at a critical point in his life and needed some guidance, and this led to a fantastic business opportunity, so Ellie was spot on. In terms of moving house, she got that right too – I have moved to the most idyllic place next to the water where it is peaceful and quiet, with lots of trees across from my house.

Georgia's indigo daughter

There are many little Ellies out there. On one occasion, I was doing a reading down in the Channel Islands where I had been for a show. The lady I was reading for, Grace, sat down and we went through the usual formalities. I asked her if she knew how readings worked, and she admitted that she had never been for one before, but had felt something at the show the night before and was now really interested in what was ahead. The first thing I saw was that her father had been killed in a building collapse many years before. Grace was shocked that I knew this, I think partly because she had never had a reading before and may have expected it to be less specific. I explained this was perfectly normal – spirit usually came and explained how they had passed so that the person getting the reading knew that it was really them. I told her that he was absolutely fine now and in a good place.

Grace's dad – George – began telling me about her daughter, who had been named after him. Georgia was about seven and her granddad doted on her. I passed on to Grace what he was saying about the little girl – that she ruled the roost, but in a nice way, as she had a great sense of humour. Her mother agreed with this and with my understanding that her daughter had been very in tune with things from a young age. She had always come out with comments which stunned the rest of the family, and also spoke of how she could see people who weren't visible to others. It was clear that she had been in contact with her maternal grandfather for all of her life.

'She has always spoken of your dad, hasn't she?' I asked Grace. 'When she was little, she would talk about the laughing man who would tease her. That's how everyone thought of your dad, as he had the great sense of humour which she has inherited.'

'How do you know this?' Grace asked.

'Well, if you want to know about the future or the past, you've come to the right place!' I laughed. 'But your daughter is a very strong character and she will be able to tell you as much as I can if she is allowed to develop as an indigo child.'

At the end of the reading, Grace asked if I would like to meet Georgia, as her granny was bringing her into town in a few minutes. I jumped at the chance. It's always a delight for me to meet gifted children and I really appreciate when their parents offer me that opportunity.

Georgia was weighing me up as she came in and I could feel that she was sensing my aura before she made the decision as to whether she would talk to me or not. Thankfully, I must have passed all of her tests. When I smiled, she smiled back.

'I've been told what a special little girl you are,' I told her.

'What do you mean?' she asked.

'Well, I know that you can see the man who is always laughing.'

She looked at her mum as if to check that it was all right to respond to this, but I also sensed that she was wondering why Grace had told me in the first place.

I tried to reassure her. 'I saw the man you can see,' I told her. 'He's your granddad.'

'Did you? Did you really?' Her face lit up. 'What did he say to you?'

'He told me that he was pleased to be able to chat and play with you because that was just the way he was with your mummy when she was a little girl. He is very happy that he can carry things on with you and that you are very special to him.'

Georgia was like the cat that got the cream. She was particularly delighted about the fact that I could share in the conversation with her.

I told Grace that whenever her little girl spoke about George she should join in too, as that would increase the bond as well as normalise what was happening.

A grown-up indigo

Some people who come for readings as adults bring with them their own skills which they have had from child-hood. I remember one man called Ian who wanted a reading, but asked if we could discuss by phone in advance how it all worked. He was very focused on the practical side and wanted lots of information. I explained to him that we would sit down and I would get out my Tarot cards, but that I would also tap into spirit and see what turned up. I told him it was simple.

'Really?' he asked. 'You think it's simple?'

'Yes, yes I do. Well, it is for me,' I replied.

'So, if someone else could do this, would you think that was perfectly simple – and normal – too?' he enquired.

The way in which he had been asking me questions and the things he wanted to know had already made me think that Ian was an indigo himself, and now I was pretty sure that the 'someone' he was talking about was himself.

'I've always been a bit … in tune myself,' he confessed, 'but I'm not sure about all of this.'

I suggested that he come along and we would take it from there. When Ian turned up, I could see instantly that he was an indigo. His eyes shone and I couldn't help but say to him, 'You have psychic eyes.'

I started by telling him a bit about indigos. He listened intently and, when I had finished, he asked: 'Is that what's been going on?'

Apparently, from a young age he had always felt like an outsider, but, at the same time, had always spoken his own mind even when this was difficult or it brought unwanted consequences. 'I never seemed to be able to help myself,' Ian told me, 'especially if someone was being picked on.' This is very typical of indigos – they will fight much more for someone else, particularly underdogs, than for themselves. He went on, 'I used to know things, but didn't know how I knew them, if that makes sense. I thought it was just me. I thought I was just odd. I was strange.'

I related to all of that. It was just how I'd felt as a child.

'I felt as if I had all the information in the world, but no one had ever told me any of it. At one stage, I thought that I had some kind of illness which troubled me so much that I began to keep things to myself in case folk would find me out.'

I think it is really important to repeat Ian's words here because, as an adult, he could look back on how childhood had been for him as an indigo and put it into perspective. If indigos are not helped through their early years because their parents and teachers have not been educated about it, everyone loses out. I didn't really do a reading for Ian; all he needed was the recognition that he was fine and actually a very special person. I wish I could give that to all crystal and indigo children. I wish I could reach out to every single one.

The 'Super Psychics'

Many people who do not see the value or reality of psychic skills are more comfortable with authority and organisation. To those people, I would ask – can you think of any organisation less likely to believe in psychic abilities than the government of one of the most powerful nations on Earth? And if that government was to put millions into researching psychic children and actually believe that they were a resource worth investing in, would that be enough to convince you? Yes? Well, it has actually been happening for years.

The 'Super Psychics' of China have been nurtured and studied for almost thirty years that we know of. Many millions have been spent on researching what is known as 'extra human function' (EHF) in children. More than 125,000 EHF children have been officially recognised and the number is growing by the day.

One of the most amazing skills which has been developed in these youngsters is that of 'psychic writing'. This involves the children being asked to imagine some written words on a blank piece of paper inside a closed pencil case. The case would then be opened to reveal the paper, and on it would be written the words the children had imagined. A little girl from Shanghai was the first to demonstrate this ability almost thirty years ago. EHF researchers then chose five more local children to train. The researchers discovered that, when blindfolded, these children were able to see with other parts of their bodies – with the ears and nose, mouth and hands, feet and tongues. And, when tested, they weren't just right some of the time – they were right *all of the time*. These children's psychic performances were flawless.

The Chinese were then challenged by American researchers. Choosing a book from an arbitrary stack, they opened it at random and tore out a page. This was crumpled up into a little ball and placed in the armpit of one child. (I guess the idea of seeing things through their armpits was the most bizarre scenario they could envisage.)

But rather than exposing wholesale cheating as the Americans expected to do, they looked on in awe as the child read *every single word* on the page.

On another occasion, 1,000 people were sitting in a theatre and each was given a single, tightly closed rosebud. A little six-year-old girl came on to the stage and, with just a silent wave of her hand, every one of the thousand buds opened into full bloom. The audience wasn't one of fellow psychics – they were just ordinary people astonished by what was happening in front of their eyes.

Another child came on and took a random sealed glass bottle of pills from a shelf of many. The bottle was placed in the centre of a table. Within seconds, the pills passed through the bottle and lay on the table. The same child took other objects, such as a coin or a pin, and made them pass back through the glass and into the bottle. I know there will be sceptics, but all of this has been independently verified by scientific journals. And given what the Chinese have been able to do with their amazing athletes, is it so unlikely that they should be able to train the mind as well as the body?

There are so many stories coming from China – stories of children who are experts at remote viewing, of a girl who can move the hands on any watch or clock without touching it, of a boy who exhibits psychokinesis. I am fascinated by it. Without this type of research or understanding, we are missing out on a huge section of life. If more countries did similar experiments, we could know so much more and experience so much more than we currently do.

Chapter 11

Seeing double

People have long been fascinated by the question of whether twins possess particularly strong psychic powers. The internet is awash with pairs who claim that this is indeed the case. Most of them seem to be American, and most of them claim they are the 'only' psychic twins around! Well, I hate to break it to them, but they'd only have to chat with me for two minutes for me to be able to prove that isn't true.

Now, as you will know by now, I believe that *all* children have psychic ability, so of course twins do too. However, some people believe that twins have particularly strong natural talents and even the ability to communicate telepathically because of the closeness they have shared since conception. Identical twins especially – created when a fertilised egg splits in two – have long been thought to be even more connected. Some people think they are almost part of each other, perhaps even sharing one soul. Non-identical, or fraternal, twins (made from two separate eggs) seem to generate much less interest in this respect.

Parents of twins often comment that, from a very early age, there seems to be a telepathic bond between them. It certainly seems to me that if two babies share a womb for nine months, then they must have a tremendous closeness. There are plenty of stories about one twin feeling pain when the other is hurt, or one female twin knowing when the other female twin is pregnant before she knows herself. Sometimes you hear of a woman having contractions for her twin sister, or a man having a clear vision about what is happening to his twin brother 1,000 miles away. The bonds are certainly strong in many cases, but does that make them psychic?

Research studies have been done on separated twins, who were placed with different families when they were babies. One of the most fascinating studies was that of Elyse Schein and Paula Bernstein, born in New York and adopted as infants by two different families. Neither they nor the families they grew up with knew it, but they were part of a secret research programme – the appalling ethical implications of which make my head spin.

The two women were reunited in 2004 at thirty-five years old, when Paula was trying to track down her birth mother. A call from a social services worker gave her the stark and incredible news that she had a live twin sister. Whatever the ethics, I do have to accept that the study presented incredibly interesting findings on the nature–nurture debate, although these came from the women themselves, not the scientists. In fact, the study ended in 1980, and the scientists involved decided not to publish their findings. Elyse and Paula are unlikely to find out what was discovered scientifically as the conclusions are in a sealed vault, where they will remain until 2066. They have had to piece together the true story themselves.

One of the people behind the study believed that twins were too often raised the same, giving them no opportunity to develop their own personalities or sense of self, and that this was psychologically damaging. What Paula and Elyse say is that they are very similar to each other, despite having had different upbringings and life experiences. Both edited their high-school newspapers and studied film at university. Both are writers, and they have always had the same taste in music and books. They have the same way of abruptly turning their heads, the same intonation and political views, the same raised eyebrows and allergies. They have identical mannerisms and tics. They are both introspective and intelligent. Whether they are psychic, I do not know, but their story raises many interesting questions. Those of you who will still be on this plane in 2066 when the findings of the study are revealed are very lucky. (I'll be watching from the other side!)

The bitter irony is that Paula and Elyse were actually dropped from the study because their baby weights were so different – but because they were settled with their new families their estrangement continued, and the findings about them will still be published with the rest of the studies in 2066.

There are plenty of stories of other separated twins which are just as striking. I've even read one report of twin sisters who were also separated at birth and found that, when reunited many years later, they had husbands and sons with the same names. I've met many sets of twins over the years. People seem to be fascinated by twins and always have questions about whether they have psychic powers.

Twin tales

Not long before I started writing this book, I met two boys through giving their mother a reading. When I was with their mum, Helen, I had a very clear connection with James and Robin but I knew that they were on this plane, not passed over. Their link was astounding, but I could also see very distinct personalities. James was a joker who loved fun and hated being bored, while Robin was very intuitive and sensitive. Helen agreed that this was the case with her ten-year-olds but wondered why they would be coming through to me if they were alive and kicking. The answer was that they were both incredibly psychic and just couldn't resist making that link with someone who would be able to pick up on them.

I told Helen about their spirit guides and the fact that they had possessed psychic abilities since they were born. At this point, four spirits came in to give me information about James and Robin, and one of them was a child Helen had lost before the twins were born. This child – a girl – was still with Helen in spirit and communicated with her brothers regularly.

'Who are the two men the boys see?' I asked Helen. Before she answered, James and Robin flashed me the words *smoking man* and *postman*. They didn't know any more details, only that both of these individuals were making regular contact with them. The links were very strong. The boys weren't there in person, but they were very chatty. They told me that they could see people inside the house and outside as they went about their daily business. It was all quite natural for them as they had never known any different.

Helen too had always accepted that they were like this and never scared them. She said that the boys talk about having *their people* around them, which I think is a lovely term. When they were stressed or concerned about anything, she explained, they'd make more of these comments and had done so since they were very little. Helen told me that once they reached the age of about seven they took a great interest in family photographs. From those, they'd identified two of 'their people', but not the *postman* or the *smoking man*. I felt strongly that these two were not part of their earthly family, but spirit guides.

James and Robin are fascinated by their gifts and, according to their mum, have often expressed an interest in developing them. I will be more than happy to help them on their journey.

My own personal experience of having twins was that they were more connected than two separate children in the family – a fact that has actually been proven so many times by so many people. For example, it was recently reported that one young girl saved her twin sister's life through telepathy. She had been listening to music while her sister was upstairs having a bath when she got a sudden urge to check on her; she said it was as if there was a voice saying, *Your sister needs you.* She went upstairs and found the other girl almost drowned after suffering an epileptic fit. When the ambulance crew arrived they said that the girl who had been in the bath had definitely been saved by her sister. Both girls confirmed that such things had been happening ever since they were little. They described each other as their mutual early-warning systems.

One of the most famous fictional examples of twin telepathy is in the novel *The Corsican Brothers* by Alexandre Dumas. The book is thought to have been based on real-life twins, as Dumas describes their abilities extremely accurately. He uses dramatic situations involving pain, sickness and death, as well as a scene in which one brother falls off his horse, thinking he has been shot when he has not – but his twin brother hundreds of miles away has indeed been killed in that fashion. Dumas may have written some wonderful stories, but he didn't have to stray far from fact when he wrote that one.

I think that there will never be any agreement about twin telepathy between those who do believe in psychic abilities and those who do not, but with so much evidence indicating that it does exist I think it takes a very closed mind to argue otherwise.

Dannielle and Simonne

My own twins always seemed to have an invisible bond and they were always in tune. Of course, they would fight like all kids, but they were connected to each other even when they did that. However, I feel that the bond goes deeper still. When my two daughters, Dannielle and Simonne, were very young, they would say things that they could not have known about. They weren't conditioned by me as I wasn't even working in this field at that time, but their comments were uncanny. They would separately tell me about the woman who sat at the bottom of their beds, reading a newspaper. From what they told me, I just knew it was my mother. I used to tell them they were so lucky to have wee angels looking over them and that this love made them special.

They used to say that *before they came down to be with me* they could see me and watched from where they were. When I asked where that was, they would point to the sky and say, *'Up there.'* Once when Simonne was very small, she was in bed with a cold. She woke up in the middle of the night with sniffles and saw a little girl at the bottom of her bed, praying – a little girl who was not her sister. She got a fright and hid under the covers. About a week later Dannnielle caught a cold and had the same experience with the same little girl, who I was convinced was an angel looking out for them. The really interesting thing is that when I was younger my sister Rita woke up one night and saw an angel praying at the bottom of my bed. I had never told my girls this story and was very touched when I realised that it was most likely to be an angel who was caring for all generations of my family.

When the twins were about six, one of their uncles died. We always used to go to visit him, and he never came to us. When he passed, Simonne asked her dad if her uncle would come and visit. My husband said 'No' quite categorically, but what Simonne had meant was that, now he was in spirit and could go anywhere, would he come to our house to visit? She knew there was no question that he would appear – it was just *where* that she was querying. In fact, the night after she asked this question he turned up at the bottom of her bed, so he did make it to our house finally after all.

Both of the girls would always say that they didn't like coming down the hallway at home, especially past my room, as there was so much psychic energy there and it disturbed them. As they got older, they were disturbed by my sons saying it was scary. As a result, Dannielle and Simonne wanted it all to stop – there was a lot of sibling pressure. Children can be very easily influenced by others and take on their beliefs, and this was what was happening. I helped them to write out a little note to spirit, which said: *We don't want to see you any more can you please stop coming!* It was plain, simple and to the point. But the important thing to take from this is that even when you are writing a note to spirit you are, at a deep and conscious level, making a choice. That's also why, when I hear of people who say they are pestered by spirit, I know that it need not happen. You have a choice and you live in this world that they are visiting, so you can say a firm *NO* and spirits need to take notice. I didn't say all of this to my little girls, but it was what was on my mind.

We left the note under the carpet in their bedroom, and from that point on it stopped. However, they have never lost their ability to tune into things and use their gift in different ways. Dannielle is very good at linking into the spirit world and has done so on more than one occasion. One night, very recently, we were sitting the kitchen chatting away and she asked me if I wanted a reading. As she started, I got such a fright. Neither of us could have predicted what was going to happen as she had never shown any signs of being talented in this way, but I suddenly realised that my daughter was a trance medium. All of a sudden her face changed, but it was what was happening to her hair that really shocked me. Before my eyes, she was turning into my mum.

When you are in the presence of a trance medium, the last thing you are supposed to do is frighten them, but I got such a shock that I jumped out of my chair (which is ridiculous, given what I do), and this jolted Dannielle back into this world. She started to relax after a while and went back to the reading as if nothing had happened. After a few moments, she turned to the side and sat the way my father always did. She spoke in his voice and answered all of my questions *as him*. I was terrified and intrigued at the same time. It was an extraordinary experience and it is apparent that she has a real talent for this type of work despite never having trained for it.

I have no doubt that her twin sister has the same abilities, but she has little interest in channelling them, so rarely goes into that part of herself. What Simonne does possess is a remarkable dream skill. Her dreams are very vivid and often come true. She has a real sense of knowing when things are going to happen, and this has been especially relevant to her career. When it is time for change, she dreams about it and it happens. She can also read tea leaves and is very skilled at interpreting the imagery in them.

Dannielle has that sense of knowing when something is going to happen – and she never doubts that it is true. She has spirit in and around her house, and often speaks of them being there as if it was perfectly normal (which it is in our family). Her ability to read Tarot cards is completely natural and wonderful to see. I feel that they are this way because it has always been portrayed as something that anyone can do. As I keep saying, we are all born with psychic ability but we make a choice about whether we use it or deny it. You don't need to be the seventh son of the seventh son, but you do need to believe and to practise.

Working with twins

My experiences as a mum of twin girls has meant that when I do a reading for another mum of twins I get a little frisson of excitement wondering what I'm going to find out.

I recently went to see a woman called Frances, who had six-year-old twins – a boy called Archie and a girl called Rosie. Frances was the sort of person who took everything in her stride, and, as a result, life had been quite straightforward for her. Archie was a quiet child, more than happy to engage with his own interests and content with his own company. Rosie, on the other hand, was energy on legs. I got this flash of demands when I worked out what she was like – *Feed me! Water me! Let me go! Hug me! Keep away! Come back!* She was always exploring things and I saw a whole episode play out, which I related to Frances.

On this particular occasion, Rosie had been at the house of a friend, while Archie stayed at home. He was upset and couldn't settle, which wasn't like him at all, as I could tell when I first looked at his character. He started crying, and when Frances asked him what was the matter he couldn't find the words, despite being a clever wee boy. As his mother held him, Archie started to rub his head, saying that it hurt really badly. 'What's wrong with it?' asked Frances. 'It hurts from when I fell off the swing earlier,' he told her – but they didn't have a swing and they hadn't been to the park that day. No sooner had he said this than Frances received a call from the mum of Rosie's friend to say that *she* had fallen off their swing and banged her head.

When I relayed this story to Frances, she confirmed that it wasn't the first time this sort of thing had happened. Archie was very in tune with his twin sister, but she was too busy going at 100 m.p.h. for anyone to notice whether she was the same about him. Not all twins are psychic. Sometimes it may only be one of them who feels the pain or upset of the other. As a parent of twins, you just have to go with the flow and allow things to be as they are.

About four years ago, I read for a pair of adult twins, Margo and Joyce. They were very different from each other (as I've said, that can happen) and only one of them appeared to be tuned in. Joyce came in to me first, and her cards were pretty much all about her love life and how it would work out. She asked me lots of stand-ard questions, which were easy to answer. I told her that her boyfriend was a saint, as she was sometimes obsessed with her work, and she laughed at this, saying she wouldn't be passing on the message if it was all the same with me!

I kept seeing her sister, which wasn't too surprising, but Margo's presence was more than would normally be expected with a sister or even a twin. It was over-whelming.

'Margo always worries about you and gets really concerned if you aren't in touch with her for a couple of days,' I said.

'She's a worry wart,' Joyce said, dismissively.

'It's more than that,' I replied. 'Margo has tremendous psychic energy. It's nothing to do with being a worry wart, but more about the fact that she really does know when something isn't right. You've had plenty of exam-ples of that, haven't you?'

Joyce went quiet. Then she said, 'A few weeks ago, she called and asked if I was all right. She said that she felt I had been upset and was very worried about me. I'd actually just had a huge row with my partner and was wondering if it was all over. I told her I was fine, but how could she have known all of this?'

It was a psychic connection between twins – no more, no less. If Joyce didn't start being honest with Margo, she risked causing her sister a great deal of stress. On the other hand, if she opened up about normal things, like how her relationship was going, she might find that her sister's psychic talents became even stronger.

The Chinese scientists who are investigating Super Psychics are also looking into the specific powers of twins and their psychic talents, and I will watch with interest to see what is discovered there. Those of us who are parents to twins are very fortunate indeed for the insights they can give us.

Chapter 12

Naughty and nice

I always like readings where I have a chuckle or when things turn out to be uplifting. Sometimes people are worried about talking to a medium, even though I try to put them at their ease, so when a bit of naughtiness or something unexpected is coming through, that can help to break the ice.

On one occasion, I got a strong impression of a child in spirit who was very unhappy. I knew that the woman I was with, Carrie, had lost a child. This little boy had been five when he passed to spirit and Carrie now had another son, William, who was about the same age. William – the one on this plane – was constantly crying. He kept telling his mum that he was being annoyed, but when he said this there was never anyone around him. Carrie thought he was simply looking for attention, but I could tell that it was Carrie's son in spirit who was contacting William. He was trying to get his brother's attention so that they could play together. The little boy who had passed over was being naughty, in the kind of way that you would expect from any pair of brothers.

When I passed all of this on to Carrie, she said that it was as if a great burden had been lifted from her shoulders now she knew that William wasn't making it all up, but she was confused too as to what to do.

'If it happens again,' I told her, 'and it will, tell William that he should let you know. Encourage him to pretend that this is his imaginary friend who just wants to play and to join in with him for a little while.'

About three months later, Carrie called me to say how thankful she was – she had done exactly what I recommended and it had made a huge difference. William was now chatting away happily, laughing and having fun. The worried little boy she had described to me had disappeared and he was settled now. I told her that things might stay that way or the connection might fade as the boy grows up, but that she should remain calm about it and accept it as natural.

I love that children who have passed still retain some of their naughtiness – why shouldn't they? They are the person they always were. It is nice when I have a reading that is uplifting or fun, as so many can be very serious and upsetting.

A lost spirit

Some years ago, I was contacted by a newspaper. The journalist told me that a family living on a council estate in Brighton had been alarmed by noises they were hearing on the stairs and it was getting worse. They feared it may be a poltergeist and wanted me to go and investigate.

I arrived at the estate with a reporter and a photographer, both of whom were clearly terrified at what might happen, the photographer in particular. I had to laugh at how a big grown man was reduced to abject terror by the thought of a ghost.

I was met by the woman of the family, who looked quite worried. She took me into the living room, where her husband was sitting with the others. I asked her to tell me in her own words what had been happening. She told me that they could hear things in the hallway, on the stairs and throughout the house. She said they were being haunted by some evil presence.

While she was talking, I was tuning into the vibration of the flat to see what would happen. I asked if I could just wander around to pick up what I could, and they agreed. The photographer was still behind me and the reporter was taking notes. As I walked through the flat I did feel an energy, but it was a playful one. Very soon, a wee girl arrived in spirit.

Hi, she said in a very friendly manner.

Using my inner voice I said, 'Hello, what's going on here then?'

Nothing, came the reply.

'Is that right?' I went on. 'Well, that's not what I've been hearing. Is it you that's been making all the noise?'

She laughed and said, *Yes, watch!*

Her spirit energy then rolled a red ball across the floor, and it did make quite a clatter. I could see why the folk in the flat would have been put out by it, if it happened from nowhere. The photographer nearly fainted!

'What are you like?' I said to him. 'If I get worried, then you can panic; but I'm fine, so you should be too.' I went back to the little girl who was in fits of laughter – I could see why. I asked her, 'Is this your family?'

No – my mummy and daddy lived here once, but they moved when I passed, she told me.

'What happened to you?'

I hadn't been well for ages and had a pain in my heart. I'd always had a sore heart.

I took from this that she had had heart problems from birth and now she was left here with no one to play with – a wee lost soul. I asked her if I could call on her spirit family and the angels to come and take her home.

She said, *I suppose so. Will it be nice where I go?*

I told her that it would be beautiful and that she would be surrounded by other angels in the heart of her family. I then called on her guardian angel and a member of her family to come and get her. No sooner had I done that than an older lady appeared. It was her grandmother, who welcomed her with open arms. I said goodbye with a lightness in my own heart, knowing that she had gone home.

After that, there was no more noise in the flat and all was well – although I'm not sure how the photographer slept that night.

On the cards

Once I was in Southampton doing a show and it was all quite heavy – I seemed to be getting a run of suicides and very dark things coming through. So I did what I always do, which is to ask spirit to come and lighten the load with some fun and humour. On this occasion, I certainly got what I asked for!

Before too long, I sensed a wee woman – even the way she came forward, waddling along, made me laugh. Anyway, there she was and I waited to see what would happen.

I'm looking for my son, she said. *Is he here? Is Peter here?*

'I don't know,' I told her. 'We'll have to find out.'

Oh, you can't miss him, she said. *You can't miss my Peter with his wee baldy head.*

I wanted to laugh at her – she was such a funny old soul – but I didn't know how Peter would feel about us all giggling at his lack of hair! I had to track him down as I was sure this lady had more to say.

'I'm looking for Peter,' I began, as the woman kept saying, *He's bald, remember, completely bald! Can you imagine it? My son – bald.* 'I have your mother here and she's a real character – she has a very distinctive walk too! Does that sound like anyone? Anyone?'

One man in the middle of the audience put his hand up.

'I think that might be me,' he said.

He was as bald as a coot so I was pretty sure it was him!

Look! said his mum. *Not a hair on him! He wasn't like that when I left him!*

I had to say something – the woman was obsessed. 'Your mum seems a bit preoccupied with your lack of hair, Peter,' I said, to lots of laughter from the audience.

'Well, I had plenty of it when she was here, so it may be a shock,' he said, in a good-natured way.

Everyone was having a good time, and the old woman was laughing too. Then, all of a sudden, she had a young boy standing beside her. '*All right, Missus?*' he said to me.

'Here we go, here's another one,' I told the audience. 'There's someone else here for you, Peter, and he's a happy soul too.' Peter was still smiling, but then I realised that what I had to say next might make his smile fade; the little boy was his son, and he must have passed when he was only about six years old.

Can you tell my dad I'm here? said the boy. *I'm with my gran all the time, and we're having a ball.*

I passed this on and, to his credit, Peter kept smiling. It was obviously an emotional moment for him, but he took it well. Then he asked, 'Is he definitely with her?'

I confirmed that he was. 'God help Heaven then,' said Peter, 'because when those two got together it was crazy. They loved each other to bits.'

The little boy told me that he and his gran played cards a lot, and that she cheated all the time.

'Nothing's changed then!' said Peter. 'Ask him if she still always gets caught because she's so bad at it.'

The boy said that was exactly what happened and that she encouraged everyone they knew to play, knowing that she'd get found out.

'We all knew, every time the cards came out, that she'd cheat – it was part of the whole thing,' said Peter. 'We had some good times. There was a lot of love back then.'

Peter had lost two very special people, but now he had been in contact with them again and he was making it obvious how much joy the whole family had generated. That was a lovely moment.

Reverting to type

I often get people coming to me because their friends have had readings, and that was the case with Alison, a woman who was based in New Zealand. Her friend had told her that I had known a lot about her family, so she booked a reading with me while she was over here on holiday.

It all began with Alison's family and some health issues that she was concerned about, and I was able to tell her that spirit were looking over her, and that it would all come good. I could see that she had considered coming back to Scotland, but would ultimately stay in New Zealand because that was where her life was now. Once we had been through the basics, as I call them, I had two children come in. They were Alison's cousins who had passed in a car accident when they were little. The eight-year-old girl was very chatty, much more so than her four-year-old sister, and her first words were, *Remind her about the time we hid her dad's teeth.*

I hate when anything comes through about false teeth because I get the feeling of them in my mouth, so I squirmed a bit, then told Alison. She was roaring with laughter.

'My God, that takes me back,' she said. 'Did you get that from my cards?'

When I told her that it actually came from the children in spirit, she got very emotional and was taken aback. I suppose she didn't expect something to come through so clearly or specifically.

'We were all close when we were younger,' she told me, 'and it was so sad to lose not just my cousins but my best friends too. Are they all right?'

I said that they were. Then the older girl in spirit came through again: *Does Alison remember when we messed up her mum's watercolour painting and she went mad? It was a picture she had been working on for ages and she had to start all over again!*

I was laughing at this and so was Alison when I told her; it really lifted the mood as it showed what little devils they had all been when they were together. It's just great when spirit give details of things that have happened which bring tears of joy and laughter, and it's always wonderful to be reminded of the fun people have in their childhood. Children love mischief, and this doesn't change when they pass over. These are the messages I really enjoy passing on.

A question of belief

While spirits can be naughty, those who have passed over also still enjoy having fun; in fact, they frequently revert to their childhood personalities. The child within them is released once they are free of earthly suffering, and this can be displayed in the way they connect with those on this plane.

During one show, I communicated with a lady called Viv, who gave me a lot of information about her condition before she passed. She left this plane after a long, debilitating illness, which affected her very badly. Viv finally told me that she'd had lymphatic cancer, and this detail helped me to get the right person in the audience – her daughter, who was there with her partner. Viv told me that she had a grandson, Tommy, who was her daughter's child. Tommy hadn't passed, but he was seeing his gran a lot. She wanted to talk to her daughter about this but it was clear that the couple were very confused. It was as if they were surprised that I was coming out with information for them, despite the fact that they had bought tickets to the show in the first place.

I gave the couple as much detail as possible about Viv, and when I told them about Tommy still having a very close relationship with her, they looked shocked. The psychic link he had with her was an amazing one, but they were not the sort of people who would take any of these messages without incontrovertible proof. I thought I had given that by now, but they wanted more.

'Your son has already told you so much of this, but you didn't believe him – let me pass on to you what he has said; and please remember that this is coming from your mother,' I said to the woman. 'He has told you about all of the mad things she used to do. He has told you about her personality and all of her likes and dislikes. You know that he was too young when she passed to have witnessed first-hand what he talks to you about. He has told you about the time that she lost her false teeth and then found them in the fridge.'

The woman burst into tears at that point, and I could see that her husband wasn't far behind. Tommy had been telling them stories about his gran for years, but they had never dared believe in them. They both now felt that there was a real connection which they could take comfort from.

'I miss her so much,' said the woman. 'She changed so much before she died.'

'Well, she is back now to how she was,' I told her. Viv's playful nature had been worn down by her illness, but since she had passed and was free of her suffering she had reclaimed her previous character and become a little girl once more, as is often the case with spirit.

Pet spirits

Links don't only exist between people after they pass; there can be amazing connections between children and pets who have gone to the other side.

I remember a woman called Lynn. At her reading, the main focus was on problems at her husband's work, until the messages moved to her two children and their characteristics. The children were not in spirit, but I could see a dog they were close to. It was a little dog, like a terrier, and there was also a black-and-white cat. The cat was like the dog, in that they both seemed to eat everything in sight. At this, Lynn laughed and agreed. I told her that they were both still very present in the house and that her two children could see them although Lynn could not. She accepted all of this, although she was a little disturbed by some things her children had told her about the pets they never knew. The children played with the pets in spirit, and I encouraged Lynn to allow this, as the animals would stay for as long as the children needed them.

I also mentioned to Lynn a recent incident in which an ornament had been broken and the children had been blamed for it, even though they'd said it was nothing to do with them. It was actually the cat who had knocked it over, and when I told her this it made Lynn recall a lot of similar incidents. Animals are very much like us in that they want to be recognised and make their presence known. Like children, or people who had a lighter side on this plane, they will be naughty or play tricks when they can.

I once did a reading where I thought that the woman worked in a zoo, because there was such a menagerie of animals with her. 'I've got a spirit zoo here!' I told her. 'They all belong to you, don't they?' She laughed and said that she just adored animals. She still had another three dogs and two cats on the Earth plane.

I don't have the ability to take messages from animals, but I can tell their characteristics and personalities. To be honest, I don't want any more; I've got quite enough with humans, but there are those who can psychically communicate with animals and their work is very similar to mine in many ways.

Chapter 13

My little friend

Younger children often stare into space. I'll be doing a reading and will see a child, one who is on this plane, and know that they are the sort of wee one who seems to just stare at the same place, seemingly at nothing, for hours on end. When I mention that, the parents generally say, 'I know – it's freaky! What's going on? It's terrifying!' But instead of getting worried about it, I wish they would just accept that their child is naturally psychically connected (as all children are) and move on. Children need their parents to allow them to be intuitive and creative; adults' fear can be what prevents children from travelling down a very natural path on their journey of life.

A long time ago, I was doing a reading for a woman who wanted to know how things would go with her job. She worked in an office where there was a reshuffle going on, and she was worried she might lose her position. I knew this wouldn't happen, and after telling her what she needed to know in that department I moved on to talk about her wee boy, Clark.

Clark was a child who was happy in his own company; he would just sit staring into space. He was also someone who would make instant decisions about whether he liked people or not. His mum laughed and said I must know him already.

'I know one thing he does,' I told her. 'He'll be sitting there, looking at nothing, then suddenly say, "Do you remember when you were little you used to ..." and will go on to describe something he couldn't have known – something you've never told him, something you've forgotten yourself until he mentions it.'

'God, you're right!' she exclaimed. 'It's amazing when he does that.'

I gave her many specific examples of times when he had used his skill to tell her things out of nowhere, things he couldn't have known. Her wee boy was obviously very much in tune and I advised her to encourage his gifts rather than be alarmed by them.

When I speak with parents of children who are intuitive or psychic, I feel that it is my responsibility to alert them to the fact that they have a special child. I love it when they see the precious qualities in their little ones. It's a natural gift, like all of the senses. Think of it in the same way as touch, sight, smell, hearing and taste, then it might not seem so alien. Not everyone is academically clever, but there are many forms of intelligence; if adults would open themselves up to the true potential of their children, they would no doubt see many more possibilities than they have ever imagined.

Tilly's little friend

Once when I went to see a woman called Carol for a reading, a little girl was sitting playing nearby. I started chatting to Carol, and was in the middle of telling her the messages I was being given when the wee girl, Tilly, came over and asked me if I would like to play. Now, although I was working, there was something about this child which drew me to her, so I asked Carol whether we could stop for a moment so that I could engage with Tilly.

'That's fine,' she said. 'I'll go pop the kettle on.'

I sat down beside Tilly and asked her what she wanted to play. 'Just whatever my friends like,' she answered. She was the only one there, and didn't even have any dolls beside her who she might have been referring to as 'friends'.

'Who's that then?' I asked. 'Who are your friends?'

'Mostly Annie,' she replied.

'And who's Annie?' I asked again.

Tilly looked at me. 'You must be able to see Annie,' she answered. 'Can't you?'

I paused for a moment because the last thing I wanted to do was put words into Tilly's mouth; I was much more interested in hearing what she wanted to say of her own accord. 'Is Annie your friend?' I enquired, not really answering her question.

'Yes. Yes, she is. She's very beautiful, isn't she?'

'What do you think is the most beautiful thing about her?' I asked, again avoiding the question.

'Well, her wings are lovely. And the way she flies. She's an angel.'

'That's lovely,' I told Tilly, as she pointed to the centre of the room. 'Look!' she told me. 'Annie's showing off, she's flying for you! Do you think she's cold?'

I asked her why she thought Annie might be cold, and was quite surprised by her answer. 'She's got no hair,' Tilly said. 'She lost it all when she was ill, and her head must get cold I think. I usually bring her one of my hats from my room but I forgot it today.' This was such a detailed thing for a child of four to say that I felt it backed up what I have always believed – that not only do children see angels, but they also communicate with them, and the angels pass on details of their own previous lives. Tilly's angel must have been a little girl who had died of cancer.

When Carol came back in, she asked how we were getting on.

'Joan can see Annie too,' said Tilly.

'I bet she can!' laughed Carol. 'You'll have to ask her to one of the tea parties you have for all your special friends, won't you?'

'I have to have the parties in this room,' said Tilly. 'They don't like it anywhere else.'

What I was very impressed with was the way in which Carol didn't dismiss what Tilly was saying or seeing. She was encouraging her intuition to grow by just allowing her daughter to chat quite normally about, and to, angels. I asked Carol if there had been anyone in the family who had lost their hair through cancer and maybe Tilly had picked up on that, but she said that wasn't the case.

'I don't really mind,' said Carol. 'She's happy; she isn't scared by any of it, and she always seems much more settled after "Annie" has been here.'

Carol's approach is absolutely the best one for parents to take. Rather than screaming, 'Oh my God! She's got angels flying about and she thinks she can see them! What am I going to do?', she just accepted it all as part of how her little girl was, and as a part of the talents she possessed. It's all too easy for parents to kill off any intuitive or psychic skill with their negativity, so I was very glad that Carol wasn't going down that route.

I could feel an energy in the room, but I didn't see what Tilly saw. That could have been because I was tuned into Carol's story and doing her reading, but it could also have been that these angels were there for Tilly and didn't want anyone else to see them. Carol told me that ever since Tilly could talk she had stared at things that her mum couldn't see and chatted away when there was no one else to see in the room. Cynics may say that children who claim to 'see' spirits have been conditioned that way, but Tilly had shown these talents from the earliest age.

'It's just the way she is,' said Carol. And she was right – what a clever and intuitive lady.

Intuition at work

Earlier in the book, I mentioned a little boy who predicted his mum's pregnancy by giving her an angel card (see pp. 29–30), and also told her that the new baby would arrive on his birthday. This little boy, Charlie, was at the centre of quite a few interesting experiences.

On one occasion, the family had been on holiday to a place where there were standing stones. Charlie was terrified and wouldn't go anywhere near them. He kept saying that he could see black people (referring to their aura, not their skin tone), and when his parents went into the circle to have a look he refused to go with them. A fire had recently been built in the middle, and even Charlie's mum could feel some sort of presence in the air. Charlie was adamant that he wasn't going in and told his parents that there were 'bad' things around the place. They heeded his advice and left.

Psychic children can encourage others around them to be more open to that side of life, and Charlie's growing skills, and his ability to see things, had given his mum an interest in reiki. One night, when Charlie and his new baby sister were in bed, she sat in their lounge, meditating. She was concentrating on what is known as the 'third eye', the spot between the eyebrows that is associated with intuition. No sooner had she started focusing than Charlie came downstairs, scared.

'Mum,' he said, 'I don't know what's going on, but my bedroom is full of eyes.' She hadn't told a soul what she was doing, but he knew.

One night, before going to bed, she peeked in on Charlie to see if he was warm and settled. As she did so, he said, very clearly, 'Mum, you're beautiful.'

'Thanks very much!' she whispered back.

'You've got gorgeous lights around you and sparkly things – and they're swirling.'

As she had been working on reiki, she knew that he was actually seeing her chakra centres – he was such an in-tune little boy and very special. I was interested when Charlie's mum also told me about 'imaginary' friends he had chatted to ever since he was very little. This is usually a clear sign of a child's gift, and one that many children experience.

Tammy and Betty

I have lost count of the number of times parents have spoken to me about imaginary friends – but because they don't understand it they either tell their children not to be silly, they ignore it or they get angry with the child.

On one occasion, I was doing a reading for a woman called Flora in Edinburgh. The first thing I got was that Flora's seven-year-old daughter, Tammy, was very intuitive and could see people. I emphasised that she might describe them as *friends* and Flora told me that it had been happening for as long as she could remember but she was still completely nonplussed by it.

'There's one woman in particular who Tammy sees, isn't there?' I asked.

'Yes – Betty,' confirmed Flora.

I could see Tammy getting her mum to set a place at the table every night for Betty, as well as insisting that there was a comfy cushion on the chair beside her bed for Betty to sit on as she watched over Tammy while she slept. I laughingly said to Flora, 'I bet all that drives you mad!'

'Actually, I'm a bit uncomfortable with it,' she told me. 'Tammy's seven now – she should have grown out of this nonsense.'

Seven! That's nothing in the grand scheme of things. I do get vexed when people try to get their children to grow up too quickly; in relation to their psychic talents, they should be hoping that they stay forever.

'She needs to stop being so silly and act her age,' said Flora.

I was horrified to hear that and a bit perplexed too. Flora clearly knew what I could do. Did she think it had all suddenly appeared to me when I was thirty? Did she think you had to be an adult before you could be psychic? When people visit a medium or psychic, they want to know that they have years of experience. They want you to have *the gift*. But where do they think that comes from? Do they think there is a laboratory somewhere cultivating psychics and ensuring that they never come into contact with 'normal' people while they're growing up? I was sitting in this woman's house at her own request, yet she was pretty much telling me that everything to do with what I believed in was odd, and that she didn't want it anywhere near her child.

I felt sorry for Tammy and didn't want her intuition to be killed off so brutally. I had no doubt that she could see Betty, and that the woman was a guardian angel for her, as well as being a good friend. A child should not be punished just because their parent doesn't know how to handle things. Anyway, I took a deep breath and went on: 'Has there been a Betty in your family at any point?' I asked.

'No, definitely not,' she replied.

'Tammy always speaks of her as having a cough – maybe you can think of someone in your family who had a bad chest? Are you sure there isn't someone? It's quite a common name.' I pressed.

'No, I've told you. There's been no one of that name.'

At her words, a woman in spirit stepped forward for me. She was absolutely indignant and I had no doubt that this was Betty. She sent me some images of her with a lovely little dark-haired girl whom I assumed to be Tammy, and I could feel the love which flowed between them. The lady told me that she was Flora's great-grand-mother. She had passed over with consumption, which is why Tammy always speaks of her cough. I gave this information to Flora, who went white and whispered, 'Lizzie, it's my great-granny Lizzie, isn't it?'

I nodded. I always tell people to think about names really carefully. Flora may always have known her as 'Lizzie' but the woman thought of herself as 'Betty'.

'I was told about her when I was a little girl. I remember doing a school project and that's when my mum told me that her granny had died of consumption. Is she really here? Can Tammy really see her?'

'Yes, she can. In fact, your great-grandmother is here right now. She loves your little girl very much; she sees herself in her. Now that you've made the link, can you please help Tammy?'

Flora was looking all around the room as I spoke, but she couldn't see anything. She had been so closed up until a moment before that spirit would never come forward to her as things stood.

'Please don't pass on your own fears to Tammy,' I went on. 'You'll kill off any gifts she has, and she's a very special little girl.'

'I'll try; I will try,' she said. 'But it's just so much to take in.'

Many parents feel that way, but if they are good people they can learn. They are usually willing to do what they can for their children in other ways – they shower them with gifts, they teach them how to ride a bike and swim, they sign them up for ballet lessons and karate, but all too often they neglect their spiritual development. I never had an imaginary friend, although I can tell you I would have loved one who could have been there for me at times when I felt alone. It's a terrifying thought to reflect on the fact that, in the past, people would have been locked up had they mentioned any of this. In fact, I wonder if we can be entirely confident that isn't still happening?

Connect yourself

There is an exercise I recommend that helps people understand imaginary friends, and can also take them back to a time when they had such a contact.

Close your eyes and make believe that you have an imaginary friend. They are very close to you. You trust them with all your heart and soul not to let you down. When you want them, all you need to do is ask them to come to you. Now, imagine that you can sense them. Are they male or female? How old are they? Do you know them, or are they someone who has just come forward for you? Ask for their name. Imagine that they are telling you about something that you need to know. Once you have all your information, thank them and allow them to go. With this, you are connecting with your own higher self and the universal consciousness that flows freely around you. You are also opening up to allow spirit to come forward as well.

This is a nice introduction to opening to spirit for everyone, and it is easy to do with children as they are so good at imaginative work. We can all benefit from opening up our minds and following the imagery which just flows.

The phrase 'imaginary friend' is just the way some children describe spirit because they don't know what 'spirit' means. Just because a child has an imaginary friend, it doesn't make them weird, strange, silly or abnormal. They can see beyond the veil, and this is a natural skill which will remain unless adults put worry into their minds. Over the last two years, I have seen such a rise in the number of people who have told me that their little one is psychic. To me, this shows that the gifts are now forcing their way through and that, try as we might to deny it, the children are actually raising the questions we should have asked decades ago.

In my mind – and in the minds of most parents, I'm sure – is the notion that when a child asks about the birds and the bees it is a signal that they are ready to know. We then use words that are appropriate to the child's age, not overwhelming them but leaving the subject open for discussion when *they* want to return to it. Why then is it so different in the case of psychic matters? Does asking about this mean any less? Is it not important? And if it's not, why are so many people scared by it?

If the child has a need to know, it is your job as a parent to fill that need. In doing so, you may be ensuring the most abundant gifts and joy in their life and, as that is all any parent really wants for their child anyway, why not?

We also need to try and avoid forming negative associations with psychic matters. Telling a child things such as 'The bad man will get you' or 'The bogey man's watching you' is not helpful. I was scared of my own shadow when I was younger and it didn't take much to set me trembling. I remember my dad saying, 'When I die, I'll come back to haunt you.' Did I need to hear that? Absolutely not. But I'm 100 per cent sure that he never meant it; for one thing, he didn't believe in 'that sort of thing'. Still, his words – if not he himself – did haunt me, and they never encouraged my psychic skills; in fact, they did quite the opposite.

Being psychic but being told to hide it is like having an unused muscle. Unless you work out, it will lie dormant – all it needs is a gentle nudge from you. I always remember seeing the film *The Sixth Sense* and thinking, 'Thank goodness someone has brought this out into the open.' It was quite brilliant the way it was done in that the main character of the little boy was seeing all these things and was terrified out of his wits because he couldn't understand what was going on. His poor mother was even worse; she had even less of a clue. But then it all made sense – and with his new knowledge and understanding came peace of mind and an ability to cope with it all.

The central premise of the film was so accurate: just ask spirit what they want, what it is you can help them with, and it will all become easier. Yes, I do see dead people, but take the word *dead* out of the equation and all I see are people who are on a different plane, much like meeting someone from another country who speaks a different language. I may need to work with them for a while to get the hang of what's happening because their culture will be different from mine, but it will come. It is all about trying to understand and persevering.

I was recently introduced to a lady whose name was Joanna. When I met her at a social gathering, she seemed to be a very open person, but there was no doubt that she was scanning everyone in the room. I recognised it well, as this is what I do myself. Once she had finished, she settled down and started chatting away, and while we waited for the others to turn up we exchanged a few snippets about how we had both come to be there and our psychic abilities.

Joanna told me that she had stayed with her cousin a lot when she was little as her mother was ill throughout her childhood. As a result, the bond between the cousins was very strong and Joanna was first made aware of her own psychic skills at that stage of her life. On top of that, her grandmother had been very intuitive and had always encouraged her to speak about how she felt and what was happening to her. She said they would talk about it for hours and it was treated as such a natural thing that she never really knew anything else.

Joanna had not used her gifts for work – she didn't see psychic mediumship as a profession – but she had found that many people would come to her and that she was able to help them by listening and giving them her intuitive insight. This is an interesting point for everyone to consider – you don't need to work as a psychic to be one. There are many ways the gift can filter through to help others.

The other point to take from Joanna's story is that it made so much difference for her to have someone to share her intuitive insight with, allowing her to grow in such a nurtured and loved way. If you are not sure how to develop your psychic child, the first crucial step is a willingness to do so; then there will always be someone, a class or information source that you can connect to that will assist further.

Chapter 14

An extended family

As we saw in the previous chapter with 'Betty', children often see and speak with grandparents and older members of the family who have passed over, in many cases before the child was even born.

Grandparents who have never met their grandchildren can feel a special connection, and there is great pleasure for them in making that link with a child they will never know on the Earthly plane. The more sensitive and intuitive a child is, the more likely it is that this will happen.

On one occasion, a man called Robert came to see me about his father, who had passed over. Robert – like many people – said that he wouldn't normally believe in 'this sort of thing', but he wanted to know that his father was all right. I reminded him that his father has already told him that he was fine, but that he had ignored it. Robert was bewildered by this and said that he had no idea what I was talking about.

His father then came in, saying: *Tell him that I've been talking to his boy – I've been chatting with Harry.*

I passed this on and Robert said, 'Harry's only four! What are you talking about?'

'Yes, I do mean that Harry – his age doesn't make any difference, and how would I know his name unless someone had passed it on to me?' I told Robert that he had already been receiving messages from his dad through Harry – the little boy had given him the knowledge that his granddad was fine, and also passed on an image of a wooden box.

At this, Robert was taken aback and began to recount his many conversations with his little boy who he'd thought was just playing. I told him that the box the little boy knew about was really significant as it held all the family documents, including his father's birth and marriage certificates. The little boy had spoken about a carved wooden box many times, but Robert had dismissed it. Belief in the connections between worlds often skips a generation – those who have passed on have to believe, as they are the ones experiencing it, and children are much more open to the messages which are sent to them.

The problem with Robert and so many people like him is the same as we have seen throughout this book: being psychic is too often seen as 'paranormal' when it should be the opposite – 'normal'. There is nothing paranormal about being in touch with your senses and feelings. Anyone who has studied ancient civilisations will tell you that all societies have had to rely on intuition in order to survive. It is only with advancements in technology that we have become lazy and dependent on getting the information we need at the push of a button. The importance of gut instinct is too often ignored or marginalised.

Iona and Daniel

I don't get angry, but I do get frustrated at the way in which lives on this plane are wasted through a lack of understanding. If only people were open to the messages that spirit are willing and waiting to give, then they would be much more settled.

I have had many experiences of situations in which someone in spirit has been waiting for years to be able to make the contact with the person on this side they want to help, but until the first step is taken nothing can change. I see it almost as a queue of people waiting with messages. They're all standing, as if they were at a taxi rank, just waiting for the opportunity to pass on love or comfort or support or warning, but until someone like me comes along to act as a conduit they're stuck.

One day I was asked to do a reading for a woman called Iona who was keen to talk about her father, who had passed recently. It was too early for her to take a message, but I was still drawn to her. She wanted the reading done at her house. I hadn't asked for any details in advance. I never ask anything because I like people to see that it's all coming through in a very pure, natural way. When I arrived, Iona made me a cup of tea while I took my coat off and got settled. As soon as she came back through from her kitchen, she burst out with, 'My dad died last month. I was absolutely devastated and I really want to know if he's all right, or I won't know what to do with myself.'

These words rang warning bells for me. Iona was very fresh in her grief and I didn't want to be giving her messages at a time that wouldn't be conducive for her. I told her this, and she looked disappointed but perked up a little when I said that I would be happy to return after some time had passed.

'Finish your tea,' she said, 'and we can just chat about other stuff.'

I had about a hundred things to do, and none of them now involved doing a reading for Iona, but I was still compelled to stay there. When I get a feeling like this, I know better than to question it; I just go with the flow.

After ten minutes or so, her son came in. Daniel, she told me, was ten years old and a very quiet boy. He smiled when I said 'Hello,' and his mum laughed.

'Don't expect him to have a natter – he doesn't like strangers.'

I'm not too keen when adults project their own perceptions onto children, as I prefer to let the child make their preferences clear. 'So, Daniel,' I said, 'how are you?'

'Are you here to talk about Grandpapa?' he asked straight away.

'Why do you think that?' I asked. 'Did your mum tell you that I was?'

He looked at her. 'No, but I just thought you were.'

'He's been saying that his Grandpapa is still here,' Iona responded, rolling her eyes.

'What?' I queried. 'Since he passed?'

'Yes, pretty much.'

'Do you want to tell me about it, Daniel?' I encouraged. 'Only if you want to, no pressure.'

'You'd think I was daft too,' he said. 'I'm not imagining things, though. I'm really not.'

'I believe you,' I told him. 'I sense people who've passed over too.'

'People who've died?' he enquired.

'If you want to call it that. I like to think that we have lots of experiences on our journey, and being in this world is only one of them. I don't think people who have died have necessarily gone. I think it's just another stage.'

The little boy looked at me. He was definitely an old head on young shoulders, and I bet, had I asked his mother, she would have confirmed he had been like that since the day he was born.

He started to smile. 'I don't talk to him. I don't hear voices. It's just …' He paused. 'It's hard to explain. It's just that I feel he's there.'

'Were you close?' I asked.

'Yes, yes, we were. I don't like talking all the time and Grandpapa would just sit with me, he didn't feel he needed to ask me questions all the time, and I was always really happy when he was there.'

'Are you sad now?' I asked.

'No, not really. Does that sound horrible?' I shook my head. 'I don't feel sad because it still feels as if he's here.'

'I feel that way too,' said Iona. 'I can't believe he's gone.'

Daniel continued, 'I actually feel that he's really still here. Not all the time, but sometimes I'll be playing or reading or watching telly when I feel different. I feel calmer, as if he's sitting beside me, saying nothing, but just being there. Do you understand?'

'I certainly do,' I told him. 'You have a special wee boy here,' I told Iona. 'He's gifted and very intuitive. I fully believe that your father is around and that he is sending comfort from the other side. I also believe that, when the time is right, you'll feel that too, but for the moment Daniel is the one he can connect with because Daniel is open to connections with spirit and actually a very settled, very stable child. You should cherish that; he'll be a wonderful person.'

Iona looked very emotional. She hugged Daniel and said that, as I had suspected, he had always been a 'sensitive' child. That is a word people often use to describe someone whose character they can't quite put their finger on and who doesn't quite fit the mould. To me, it's not an insult, it's a compliment, and I really hope that Iona gloried in her son's talent and took comfort from it. Her father obviously recognised the beauty in the boy. The bonds between grandfather and grandson were so strong that their understanding went beyond this plane, and if Daniel continued to be open he would find these bonds strengthened even more as time went on.

Reading a photo

I feel there are two major factors that stunt the intuitive development of children. One is parents and peers who don't understand what psychic skills really are; the other is the school environment, where creativity is timetabled and everything is prescriptive. Intuition is a natural skill that everyone has, regardless of their academic ability, and children who seem to fall outside the narrow confines of 'clever' should be looked at to see if they hold other talents. My aim is to help and assist these children and parents in developing their psychic ability and using it in ways that help their own lives.

Too many folk watch too much television and it wreaks havoc with their imagination. It gives them a completely distorted view of what being psychic is about. I met a woman called Clara, who said she had been for a lot of readings, but still didn't 'believe'. She told me some of the things other mediums had given her, and I was amazed at how detailed and accurate the information was – but it still wasn't enough for her.

'I would love to know how you do what you do. How does it all work?' she asked.

Ah! I thought. It wasn't about the accuracy of the message, it was about the process.

'I want to know something about a person in a photo I have,' she went on, 'but I suppose you won't be able to tell me anything if I don't have it with me.' I was ready for that, as I could see she was quite a sceptic.

'It's no problem at all,' I told her. 'I can see him quite clearly. Do you want me to start?'

Clara seemed taken aback that I knew it was a man, but quickly recovered. Knowing that she was so sceptical, I realised that she probably thought I'd had a fifty–fifty chance and had got lucky with my guess. 'Don't tell me anything,' I said to her, 'just wait and see.' Richard came through very quickly and I described his characteristics. However, I started to feel very, very sick without warning. I felt compelled to take off my shoes and my glasses, and had no idea why this was the case. It was as if someone was demanding that I do it. As I chatted to Clara, while removing these things, I said to her, 'This is obviously important.'

'You have no idea just *how* important,' she replied.

It wasn't normal, but I pushed it aside as Clara's granny came through (those who have passed to spirit often see those they have left behind as the children they were when they passed). I thought she was telling me about the war when she said, *Just tell her about the tin helmet.* I did and Clara smiled, saying that was 'right'. 'Tell me later,' I said, 'because it doesn't make sense to me just yet.' I had to give her a name, but wondered how she would react. 'I know you're a sceptic,' I began, 'and Lily is quite a common name, but I can only give you what I get and there's a Lily here.' I could tell by her face that it was all going well.

At the end, I said to her, 'Go on then – how did I do?'

Clara laughed. 'Not bad,' she said.

Now it was my turn to be surprised. 'Not bad? What did I get wrong? Was it Lily? Not specific enough?'

Again, she smiled – but I had a question to ask her. What was going on when I'd felt compelled to take off my glasses and shoes?

'Richard was a radiographer,' she told me, 'and he always had to take everything off before he went into the old-fashioned screening room. That would be him passing that on to you to let me know he really was there.'

Clara got up to leave and, as she did, I knew what I needed to say. 'Lily! That's your maternal great-granny, isn't it? Are you happy now?' I had a very clear voice in my head at that stage with Lily saying, *Don't forget to tell her who I am.*

What had happened with Richard often occurs – when I'm doing a show, I have so many things passing through that it is often the strong physical sensations which make people realise I have messages for them. I may limp, cough or develop an accent.

Once I started dragging my leg across the stage when a man came through. He had been in an accident and his foot had got caught in a machine, with his boot still on. As soon as the message from him had been passed on, I was fine. Things like that don't hurt, but they are uncomfortable. I also really hate when they have false teeth as I have that sensation in my mouth while I'm communicating with them – I'm always glad to get rid of that!

Some children will give me toys – but not every child is playful or fun. If they are musical, they might place a guitar in my hands. Usually such details not only bring emotion, but feelings of relief – often tears. I always say that if it's too much I can stop, but no one has ever asked for that. They want to know, they want reassurance, and they want the contact.

The lady with the sad face

I was at a house reading cards for a woman and her friends when a woman called Irene came in – she hadn't planned to be there for a reading, but there was someone in spirit who communicated with me immediately, so I could only think that they had been waiting for a chance for a very long time. They wanted to talk about Irene's five-year-old granddaughter, Jemima, so I let it all flow.

'She's a scream, isn't she?' I laughed. This girl's energy was so light that I felt lifted as soon as she came through. 'She could be on the stage, that one – she entertains everyone!'

Irene said that I was absolutely right – but how did I know?

'There's someone looking out for this busy wee girl – your mum.' Irene's mum had actually passed to spirit many years before Jemima was born, but the two had a strong link. 'Your mother could be a very serious woman, couldn't she? She found it very hard to relax and let things be.' I verbalised the image which was coming into my head. 'She was like a dog with a bone sometimes.'

'Yes, that was my mother!' said Irene.

'She's around you, but you already know that – Jemima has told you, hasn't she?'

Irene looked taken aback. 'How do you know that?' she asked.

It makes me laugh when people say that – what do they expect? The lady in spirit, Irene's mum, told me that Jemima often told Irene that the *lady with the sad face* (Irene's mum) was there, but that she was going to put on a show for her to cheer her up.

'That's absolutely true,' Irene said. 'Is she putting on the shows for my mum?'

I told her that was exactly what her daughter was doing. Jemima was a very tuned-in little girl who had always spoken about her grandmother since she could talk, and the relationship was still there between them even though one had passed. Irene was delighted because she said her mother would have loved Jemima and that she just knew they would have had a great time together. I told her that actually they already were having a great time. I felt the great-grandmother was having a ball with this bundle of fun who had finally shown her how to relax.

Animals in the family

Sometimes people have animals in their extended families. Now, as I've said, I'm no animal psychic, but they do come through in spirit at times, although they never fancy much of a chat!

On one occasion, I was reading for a woman who I sensed was very into the country life and horses. I told her that there was a horse in the spirit world, but also that she had a new one which was a recent purchase. She agreed. I said, 'When you go to the stables, the new horse is sometimes up against the far wall, isn't he?' She looked surprised but agreed. I said that the spirit horse used to be in that very place and its presence was still there. She cried a bit, then said that she thought it was just her that felt it and that she was worried about telling anyone else in case they thought she'd gone mad. I told her that for the new horse to be able to have its place and be part of what she wanted it to do, she needed to speak to the old horse and allow it to move on.

A couple of months passed, and I bumped into the woman again. She told me that she had done just as I suggested and the new horse had taken its place and was not pushed against the wall any more.

You know, writing this book has been an eye-opening experience for me, because collecting all of these stories has shown me just how desperate spirit is to make contact and how defiant we are about not accepting it at times. When I get up in the morning, I wouldn't say that I take my gift for granted, but I do think that I'll give readings and they'll 'work'. Putting it all down on paper has made me see how every single interaction is a little miracle.

Anna's gift

I was recently doing the cards for a woman called Donna, and it was apparent that her twelve-year-old girl was highly intuitive. I told Donna that Anna, the child, always tunes in to things and she is completely at ease with spirit – she agreed with all of that.

When Anna was two and a half, she had been sitting chatting away to herself as usual. Donna asked her what she was doing and she said she was talking to the lady. 'What lady?' asked Donna.

'Your grandma,' replied Anna, as if her mum was asking a pretty daft question in the first place. Now, Donna's grandma had died long before she herself was born, so she knew nothing much about her. 'She died when she fell down, you know,' said Anna. Donna dismissed this as the chatter of a little one's imagination, but it preyed on her mind, especially when Anna kept saying she was chatting to the lady.

The next time Donna visited her dad she asked him what he could remember about his mother. 'Where do you want me to start?' he asked. She told him just to tell her anything. 'It's still hard to talk about her,' her dad said. 'It still hurts that she was taken away from us so suddenly. If she hadn't had a stroke and fallen that day, she might have lived to see your wee one being born.'

Donna was shocked – her grandma had died after she fell from a stroke, as Anna seemed to know. She went back home and wondered what she would say to Anna. She needn't have worried about what to do; the little girl seemed to know that the questions had been asked. As soon as Donna went in, Anna ran towards her. 'It's all right,' she said, 'the lady will look after you – she'll look after the baby too.' It turned out that Donna was pregnant and her wonderful little daughter had discerned it before she knew herself.

Some time later, Anna came into her mum's room and said, 'Can you tell the man who is sitting on my bed to get off?' Obviously, Donna hadn't quite learned her lesson because she told me that she was just 'humouring' her daughter when she went into her room and chided, 'Come on now, get off the bed,' into thin air.

Anna said, 'No, Mummy, tell him properly.'

Donna paused. 'Who is this man?' she asked.

'Your grandfather,' said Anna. 'But it's all right; he'll listen to you. You can call him Marty, if you like, but don't laugh about his hand – he only has one. He's nice, though, when he isn't being naughty.'

'Where does Marty come from?' asked Donna, finally going with the flow.

Anna pointed up.

'The loft?' asked Donna.

'No, silly! The sky,' she replied.

Again, Donna asked her father and every detail was correct, right down to the missing hand.

When Anna was seven, she was at Donna's bedside one night while she slept. Donna woke up with a scream when she saw her daughter had a man in spirit with her. Anna was scared by her mother's reaction, and it worried her so much that they both asked spirit not to come any more. Once Anna was twelve, however, she decided to revive her talent and start communicating with spirit again. I have no doubt that she will do brilliantly at it and I'll be hearing from Anna very soon.

International developments

Anna is the sort of child who would benefit from some of the wonderful developments which are going on around the world. In the States, the home of the summer camp, there are even programmes for psychic children to take during the school holidays. Since 1999, camps have been held in the Appalachian mountains for those endowed with psychic talent. During these weeks, they are encouraged and helped to develop their spiritual intelligence in a loving, nurturing environment and their inner senses are brought out.

I would love such courses to be available to all children, and some recent news stories suggest that it may soon be more than the stuff of dreams. Recent research suggests that lots of us are blessed with this ability. In November 2010, the *Daily Mail* reported about a study by a respected psychologist into these phenomena. This sparked lots of conversations about the significance of everyday occurrences.

In one experiment, students were shown a list of words to memorise and later asked to recall as many as they could. Finally, they were given a random selection of the words to type out. It was found they had more skill in remembering some words than others, and amazingly these tended to be the words on the list they would later be asked to type, suggesting a future event had affected their ability to remember.

This is the sort of media coverage which really excites me because, once things are accepted in the mainstream, perhaps children will stand a chance of being taken seriously. So many are just ignored, dismissed or even punished when they 'see' things, but if Mum or Dad happened to read a newspaper article that day which made them wonder about it all, maybe they'd think twice.

When problems arise

In the majority of cases, when a child is seemingly staring into nothing then laughing and chatting, it is a perfectly normal occurrence and should be treated as such. Parents should not worry about 'fixing' a 'problem', as there is nothing to *fix*. If they are happy, then let them be. If, however, there is a problem, then it would be appropriate to find out what the problem is and ask an expert for some help. If the child is unhappy with their gift, or it is causing them distress, you should seek the advice of a professional medium, who can assess the issues and make suggestions about what could be done. If it is felt psychic intervention would help then this can be done as well.

I knew one young boy called Michael who would sometimes see spirit. He was not very comfortable with it, which was why it did need some 'action'. He used to see his grandfather standing in the room in the suit he was buried in. Michael told his mum to tell the grandfather not to come and see him as he was scared. She did this, and it stopped; I feel that this is because he just closed off to it and because his mum did the right thing.

Another child, Jane, had always been psychic. She had seen things since she was small; she had grown up with this and was used to spirit in her life. However, one night when she was a young woman she was sitting with her aunt, who was a medium, chatting about psychic things, and the two of them were giving each other readings. Jane started to tell her aunt information about her gran that was so accurate her aunt could hardly believe it. What was most amazing was that Jane's facial features changed as she spoke, and it was as if her hair was different too – it was thick, light and wavy. Jane sat back and chatted some more and began taking on the mannerisms of her uncle this time. It got so uncanny that her aunt became frightened, which brought Jane back into this world, so to speak. Jane had a natural ability for trance mediumship but was afraid that she would not be able to control it or control what came through and she wasn't sure how she would get rid of it again, so she stayed away from it. This is a shame, as it can be a wonderful talent if channelled correctly.

The imagination is such a powerful tool that it can make you create and bring forth all manner of things. The truth is, as long as you believe that only positive good can come through, then that is all you will get, but you need to make this decision and there can be no faltering from it. Children and young people are so naturally gifted in intuition and psychic ability that we need only support them and assist their progress. This is not difficult; it is about letting them know it is all right to tap into their skill and that they can do anything they want, if they choose. It's about building their confidence and trust. Children are very good at picking up on energy and spirit and will come out with the most amazing information if they are given the chance.

Chapter 15

Angels, gatekeepers and secrets

Many children who have passed over become guardian angels or spirit guides to the family they have left behind. Guardian angels are thought to be assigned to us all at birth. We each have one, but some of us have more than one and they can come in and out of our lives at different times and for different purposes. We may need a guardian angel to get us through one part of our life experience when we are twenty, but a completely different one five decades later. It doesn't matter if you don't believe in guardian angels – you have one anyway and there is no getting away from it. They may work through inspiration or through leading us to safety, maybe through luck or coincidence, or even through bringing a miracle to our door. Many of the things in our lives that simply cannot be explained have the light touch of a guardian angel behind them.

Guardian angels do what they can, but they won't help out in instances where they think they are being asked for something which does not truly benefit the person. They are more likely to respond to spiritual requests and those which will enhance your growth and emotional wellbeing than to bring you a diamond ring or a new dress.

In one case, I was doing a reading for a woman called Laura, who was so distraught over the loss of her child that she was still grieving many years later and had not moved on. She had kept the little one's room exactly as it was before she passed away and it was all having a very bad effect on her and her family.

When I started to read for Laura, I got a very strong sense of her child, Sophie, being in the bedroom, which is where I was doing the reading. The corner next to the window buzzed with spirit energy and Sophie was desperately trying to get my attention.

Laura told me that every night she could feel Sophie in the spot I told her about. As I connected with Sophie, the little girl told me, *My mummy is very sad and I don't like it. She's always crying. I want her to feel better. I want to make her better. I try to let her know that I'm here, but she can't see me.* I asked Sophie how she tried to let her mum know she was there. *I move things,* she said. *And she knows it's me, she smiles – but I wish she could see me.* I asked Sophie if she was there for any reason other than to let her mum see her and she quickly replied: *Yes, she's not well. Mummy needs to go to the doctor – she needs to go very quickly.*

Sophie was very agitated when she said this and added that she'd tried to get Laura's attention by knocking things down and breaking them, but it wasn't helping. She also revealed that Laura is in an abusive relationship which is getting more violent, and that there have been many times when she has watched her getting hurt very badly.

This was a tricky situation for me – I had to weigh up the consequences of telling Laura that I knew something so very private, but felt I had a duty to encourage the woman to seek help.

Thankfully, Laura admitted everything, and while she said she didn't have the courage to leave her partner or seek help she did agree to visit the doctor the very next day, where it was discovered that she had diabetes. While there, the doctor noticed how badly bruised she was and, feeling the strength from her daughter, Laura opened up about what had been happening.

When I met Laura again two years later, she was a changed woman. The messages she had received from her little guardian angel had altered the course of her life. Her health problems had been addressed, she had left her abusive relationship and she was training to be a bereavement counsellor for parents who had lost a child. Her guardian angel Sophie had done a marvellous job.

Getting in touch with guardian angels

When people talk of angels, guardian or otherwise, it brings up certain images. We all have our own ideas what they look like and there are so many stories, myths and legends around them that they permeate our culture. Some people have said that they have heard their guardian angel and that the sound is a musical one; others have claimed that they have felt them at their side, and that the sudden warm sensation or comfort that envelops them is proof of an angelic presence. It has been reported that angel wings cause light breezes to flutter in still surroundings, and that white feathers are often found when one has passed by or when they want to leave a message that they have been close.

Whether you call them guardian angels or spirit guides it really makes no difference in the scheme of things, so long as the correct help and information get through. Sometimes children who pass might be classed as angels, while older people are seen more as spirit guides. The difference is only in the name, term or label you decide to give them.

There are many ways in which you can try to contact your guardian angel. Here are some suggestions:

- Clear your mind – your guardian angel won't be visible or audible if you are too busy. Make yourself comfortable

– decide whether you feel better sitting or lying down. Let your body become limp and relaxed. Empty your mind and just be. Tell your guardian angel that you wish for contact – and wait.

- Ask a direct question in your mind and you will be more likely to get a direct answer, perhaps in a daydream.
- If you don't believe, or think it's all a big joke, you won't get contact – why would they bother?
- Write a letter to your guardian angel – tell them how you feel and what you need. Put it under your pillow or in a special place.
- Visualise your guardian angel – try to see them in your mind's eye and be open to the images that occur.
- Try speaking aloud – it may help you focus.
- Notice new lights or colours, feelings or sensations – all of these can be indicators that your guardian angel is there.

When psychics work, they sometimes refer to their guide who brings spirit through – they are there as the gate-keeper, to ensure that only the spirits on a certain level are allowed in. I made a personal decision a long time ago only to work with spirit on a higher plane; this doesn't mean that I'm a psychic snob, but that I will not work with lower-level entities. I want the good, energetic souls, those who are in need of getting a very important message over to loved ones to let them know that they are all right and to give them comfort. I feel that for me, those on the lower plane would drain my energy and leave me weak in my work, and I have not come this distance in my journey to allow that. I have seen the ways in which some mediums and psychics who do allow this have constant health problems. They wonder why this is the case, but it seems perfectly obvious to me – you are what you live, and if you allow badness in there will be repercussions.

'The work of the devil'?

One day, I read for a woman who was shy and not very high in energy; she was a nice person but you could see she had been through the mill in her life. I opened the reading with information about her relationship, and this made her clam up, as if it was not to be spoken about. I asked her if it was a subject she would rather I stayed away from. She was unsure, I could see, so I suggested that I continue but that if it got too much I would stop. She nodded in agreement.

I went on, and told her about her son, Connor, who was a lovely little boy, but who, like her, was quiet. I told her that he was very psychic, at which the woman almost had hysterics. I said it was fine, and I continued because she needed to hear this. 'Connor always speaks to his friend on the other side,' I told her, 'and he has spoken about his angel.' She nodded, almost afraid to smile. The problem lay in her husband, a very religious man who thought this was all mumbo jumbo and the devil's work.

I could see that theirs was a tough household and that things like this were never discussed as her husband wouldn't like it. She agreed, but I said Connor was special and he should be nurtured.

She leaned over to me and said, 'You're preaching to the converted.' I didn't expect that. 'I know what it's like to be that way,' she said. 'I have been all my life, but I dared not mention it for so long. My parents were religious, and now I have married into the same – what's this all about?'

There was a lesson here, but it was not about her husband – it was about her. She needed to let go of other people's fears, believe in herself and be happy. In turn, so would her son, if she allowed it, but I think she already knew that. It's sometimes not about the reading, but more about the chat that flows through and around it. This can allow the necessary changes to happen for people so they can validate what they already think is so. I'm not there to tell people what to do in life; I'm only the messenger that provides a safe space for spirit to come and provide them with information. The rest is very much up to them and what they do with it is their own path and business.

This concern about bad spirits or devils is an interesting one; I don't believe that you need to take on anything you don't want, but it can worry some people. I was once asked to do a reading for a young boy called Adam. When I found out he was seventeen, I said that unfortunately he was too young. Then, a little while later, his mother called me. She said that Adam had always been psychic, but that it could sometimes be a real burden because he would experience really vivid dreams and get the sense that his whole bed was shaking. 'He can be quite disturbed by it,' she said. This was interesting. She told me that he sometimes had dreams that he was in the war as well.

I began to tell her some things which struck me, one of which was that I sensed the boy had been in this type of environment in a previous life and he was reliving it. She said Adam was always fascinated by history, especially things to do with the First World War, so that made sense. I also told her that I felt his grandfather's presence around him and he had been in the Forces – again, this was correct. The boy was obviously channelling quite a bit, but not sure of how to control and use his skills.

I told her that if Adam was afraid, the first thing he needed to do was to ask his gatekeeper or spirit guide to keep out negative entities and take control of it for him. He should do this every night before he went to sleep. The other thing I asked them to do was to leave an open Bible next to Adam's bed. Whether you are religious or not, it makes no difference – the Bible (or any holy book, as long as it has pure connotations) acts as a positive amulet for protection; it acts as a barrier to negative influences, at least until the person is in a place to be able to do this for themselves.

Your gatekeeper is your warrior who should be on call should the doorbell go and you don't know who is there. Let them answer it and make the judgement call on your behalf. But make sure that you have told them the type of things you do and do not want. You are in charge.

It was Shakespeare who said that all the world's a stage and all the men and women merely players, but we are all playing our own role in a connected universal consciousness, and if we acknowledge this we can feel better and more able to connect beyond the veil. The energy boundary is very thin; as long as you are willing and open, there is no reason why you cannot connect with your loved ones on any other plane.

People often think this is all very mysterious, but it doesn't have to be. Guardian angels and spirit guides and gatekeepers are wonderful, but they don't have to be shrouded in mystery. If you want real mysteries, the secrets spirits reveal will give you that. The people I have met over the years have so much in common – they all seek comfort, support, and the recognition that no one is alone. We don't exist on this plane without the help of those on the other side, and when people pass they don't disappear into nothingness. So often I am asked: Will there be someone to meet me when I pass? Will one of my loved ones help me through? Or, do they know I love them? Do they know that I wished I'd been there? I've lost count of the number of people who have had a loved one in hospital, then popped home to get something, only to find out that their parent or child has passed while they have been away. They want the person to know. If someone has been in a coma, the loved ones want to be assured that their presence was recognised.

The answer is always the same: when someone passes to spirit, the knowledge is always there. Everyone needs comfort and reassurance, and that works for both sides. Those in spirit want to give it, those of us who remain on this side want to receive it. When I hear a sigh of relief from either party, then I know my work is done. The communication brings a settling and people can move on – not forget, but move on.

A message from Rachel

There are some instances where things can be brought up once contact is made that no one could have expected. Sometimes the spirit world chooses to reveal secrets that many have been kept buried for many years.

I met with one woman called Yvonne for a reading after her daughter, Izzy, had organised it as a birthday gift. This woman came across as a very cheery soul, but I could tell that it was a front. She had a sadness inside that was glaringly obvious to me and I suspected immediately that the reading would reveal something which would make sense of that.

I was right. As soon as I began, a child from spirit came in. 'It's your daughter,' I told Yvonne.

'What? Are you sure?' she asked.

'Absolutely,' I replied.

'Does that mean she's going to die?' panicked Yvonne. 'Does that mean that Izzy is going to die? I can't lose Izzy, I just can't!'

'Izzy's fine,' I reassured her. 'Izzy isn't going anywhere – this is your other daughter.'

'What? I don't have another daughter. I don't have any other children, I only have Izzy,' Yvonne insisted.

The daughter she had in spirit was as real as she was, but this was obviously a sensitive matter. 'Is it all right for me to go on?' I asked. Yvonne actually looked torn as to whether she wanted to hear what I had to say, but eventually she nodded. 'Yes,' she said. 'I need to hear this – will it be all right?' she whispered.

'It'll be fine. Whatever this is, I'm sure it will help,' I said. I'm always very careful not to push people in situations where I feel that the information coming through is distressing rather than comforting, but I was faced with a dilemma here. The child desperately wanted to make contact, but her mother was very upset. All I could do was go on my gut instinct; I had felt that Yvonne was putting on a front as soon as I had met her, and I suspected that the message I had for her would get to the root of it. I also knew that the child in spirit meant no harm; I sensed a loving energy and I went with my intuition to give Yvonne the reassurance that all would be well. The girl sent me her name and I said, 'Hello, Rachel.'

Yvonne became upset again as soon as those words left my lips. 'I can't believe this. I can't believe this is happening. Is it really her? Is it really Rachel?' she asked.

I was getting very clear messages – Rachel had been waiting a long time for this moment. She was a little girl in the vision I received, but passed on the fact that she would have been thirty years old on this plane had she survived. She told me that she had been put up for adoption when she was little. I passed all of this on to Yvonne, who was becomingly increasingly upset.

Please help her, said the little girl. *Please help my mum.*

After I had calmed Yvonne down as much as I could, she told me the full story. At seventeen she had become pregnant but knew that her family would never support her. As a result she moved away to a big city, and they never knew anything about the pregnancy. She gave birth, named the little one 'Rachel', and made the heartbreaking decision to give her up for adoption. Yvonne told me that she always loved her deeply, even though she was only with her for a week or so; she'd thought she would never get over parting from her baby, but the adoption agency had found a lovely family for Rachel and she'd received regular updates until the wee one was three.

'I remember the call to this day,' she told me, shaking. 'The agency was so good – they never made me feel like a bad person, they never made me feel as if I should be punished, and they always let me know what stage Rachel was at, when she started talking and walking, things like that. Her new family was lovely and I knew that she would have all the chances in the world with them – but I never suspected for a moment she would get ill. They called me on a beautiful bright winter's day and told me that she'd died of pneumonia. I thought my heart was going to break the day I handed her over, but I knew now that was nothing compared to the reality of never being able to see her again.'

I cried myself at her story. Yvonne seemed such a strong woman, but I was angry at the fact that she had even considered that anyone would think her a bad person who should have been punished for giving her child up. I was overwhelmed by the emotion of the whole story.

'Rachel is desperate for you to know that she loves you and always has loved you,' I told Yvonne. 'I know that you are aware of the fact that her adoptive parents never changed the name that you gave her, and that she was always known as Rachel, but do you know that she has been with you in many ways since she passed?' In fact,

Rachel told me that she had *always* been with her mother and that she felt a tremendous link, not just to her, but to her sister, Izzy, too.

'When you came in, Yvonne, when I told you that I could see your daughter, you said that you only had Izzy …' I reminded her.

'I know, I'm so sorry. Can you tell Rachel that I'm sorry?'

'She knows – she's here!'

'I just thought that she had gone and that Izzy was the only one I had left, and I felt so guilty again,' she said.

'There's something else, isn't there?' I coaxed. 'Something happened last week, didn't it?'

'How do you know that?' she asked.

'Rachel knows. Rachel told me,' I replied.

The week before our reading, thirty years after she had given birth to her first daughter, Yvonne had finally told her family about the little girl. Her parents, daughter and husband had all been shocked, but had rallied round. Despite the love she was surrounded with, Yvonne still felt empty. The loss of her baby all those years ago had taken its toll and she never felt at peace. To the outside world, she was a confident, happy woman, but inside she was always sad.

'You don't have to feel that way any longer,' I told her. 'Last week, it was as if you felt you had to free yourself of the burden you have carried alone for so long. Rachel has always been with you and she was with you as you told your family about her. It was she who encouraged you to share your terrible despair over what happened, and that's why you finally felt the pressure to tell.'

We spent the rest of the reading with Rachel and I felt so lucky to have been part of that reunion. When Yvonne left, she was a different woman, and I knew that for her, and for Rachel, this had been one of the most important times in their existences. Rachel was her mother's guide, who would help her through her life, and the energetic bond between them would always be strong.

There is no better way to learn than to embark on a journey of discovery; it can only be amazing if you let it unfold. In the early days, when there was no one to whom I could turn, I did a lot on my own to dig and try to find wee gems and nuggets of help and information. It was hard, but it was all very much part of my apprentice-ship and I wouldn't be here telling you this story if I hadn't taken up the gauntlet.

It is lovely when you find people who are of similar mind to yourself and who can share their gifts and stories, but no two people are the same; we all experience things in a different way, and that is part of our uniqueness and beauty. Some people are good at clairvoyance or the gift of second sight, but the truth is that to develop these gifts all you need to do is focus on what's already working for you and build it up.

When I started along this path, I wasn't brilliant at seeing, hearing and sensing; it all took its natural course and, as I grew and new spirit guides came along, I would feel the change and sense new skills being sharpened.

So if you need a word of advice, I would say: please trust what you have, and develop the rest. Don't look for what you don't have; instead, focus on what works, then when you have that all in place your gifts and skills will evolve.

I am confident that we are all assigned a belief guide who helps us along the path of life we choose and who has our best intentions at heart. They will never lure you into anything that is negative. At various stages along the way, the guides do change, and the reason for that is that they have done their work and taken you to where you needed to be. It's a bit like school − it would serve no purpose if you were to have the same teacher the whole way through. The belief guide also needs to grow, and in assisting your progress they assist their own.

Earth angels

I want to reflect for a moment now on earth angels. I feel hundreds and thousands of them walk the planet. My children have been my earth angels, who have supported me in everything I've done, taught me and given me laughter. There have been many others along the way too.

Whenever someone is speaking to you, they should get a message from you and you from them, because we are all connected to the universal consciousness. You may be chatting generally to someone about an issue in their life and suddenly realise that the conversation applies to you as well. This frequently happens to me when I am giving readings. When I pass on a message at a show, it may be that other members of the audience apart from the person the message is intended for will be helped by it. We are all connected, so there is no reason at all why we would not get a message in this way.

How many times have you been stuck or in the depths of despair when, out of nowhere, a stranger or kind passer-by came along just when you needed them? Your call had been heard on some level and was echoed back to you by their appearance. There are countless stories like this of people who were helped by earth angels; some have turned around to thank them, only to discover that there was no one there. They are a gift from above.

As this book moves towards its close, I would like you to look out for guardians and angels – they are all around you, and I would like to think that I have helped you to recognise them. I hope you are sprinkled with angel dust today, and that you share it as you continue on your journey.

Chapter 16

Reflecting and learning

I am often asked for advice on dealing with children who are showing signs of psychic awareness. If you are blessed with psychic children yourself, then there is much you can do to help them. The aim of the games in this chapter is to provide you with some simple tools to help your child develop their natural skill of intuition and have fun at the same time. The games are also meant for adults to join in because, this way, you will grow intuitively together. There are a couple of rules to remember: keep it simple and remember that it's not about concentration; intuition will flow naturally if given the chance. Also, if possible, keep charts and points. This will encourage your child and help both them and you to build trust in what you are doing. When you can see it in black and white, it becomes tangible, and it also has the added element of making the children competitive, and they just love this. The more you build this up, the better; encourage them to see how well they can compete with friends and family, so long as it's all in good fun – anything else turns it into the left-brain logic and takes away from intuition.

These simple techniques should allow your child to tap in easily to their own intuitive potential allowing it to flow naturally.

The 'Disney' phone game I mentioned on p. 173 is only one of many fun things you can try. Here are some more:

Which country?

For this, you will need:
- A large map of the world
- Cut-outs of people from different countries (you can do this by cutting up magazines or travel brochures – it's something for you to do, not the child)
- Envelopes
- A notebook

Lay the map out on a flat surface, such as the floor, kitchen table or worktop, and decide which person and country you want to focus on – this decision is yours, not the child's, and they should not see the picture of the person. Once you have done this, place the cut-out of the person in an envelope and put it somewhere safe.

Now, the child has to find the country which they think the person comes from by running their hand over the map. You can help them by telling them that their hand is getting hotter when they are near to that country, and colder when they are a long distance away. They might also tell you that they have a feeling about the colour of the person's skin, the type of food they eat, how they dress and so on. Start a points system and jot down in your notebook what they say and how accurate they are.

This game not only develops intuition; it also helps with your child's knowledge of world geography and social skills. The only thing you need to do is make sure you know the right answers in advance!

Which card do I have?

For this, you will need:
- A deck of playing cards

This is like a guessing game for children. Take out all of the face cards from the pack, then shuffle the rest. Now, select a card and ask your child what colour they think you have. Then ask them the suit. As they become better at guessing the correct ones, return the face cards to the pack and see if they can guess which one of these you have chosen. Keep a chart so that they can plot their progress and yours as well. You can extend this to include their friends and how well they do, so that it becomes a competition.

What's in the bag?

For this you will need:
- A bag of some description
- A selection of items to fit in the bag

The idea of this game is to place an item in the bag and let your child guess what it is, using their intuition. They are allowed ten tries to reveal the hidden item. Keep a note of their answers and award them a point for each one they get right. Once they have finished one cycle of guessing, try again with another item. You can do this as often as you like. In fact, why not turn it into a family game and see who gets the most points? This is also a really good party game.

What's in the picture?

For this you will need:
- A selection of photographs

It's amazing what secrets a photograph holds; it can tell you a lot about a person if you look closely enough. Ask your child to look at a picture of a friend or family member and tell you what they think the person in it is really like. Ask them if they think the person is a happy or sad individual. Are they good fun to be with or are they serious? Make up your own list of questions for each person and see how they get on. Children are far more intuitive and perceptive than most adults, and you may be surprised by what they say, especially with people who passed on before they were born or before they were old enough to know them. If your child reminds you of someone, perhaps a beloved grandparent, then find a photograph of them that they haven't seen before and see how much they can pick up on from that one. This can be quite an emotional game for the adult.

Creative box of secrets

For this you will need:
- A small cardboard box with a lid
- Comics
- Magazines
- Scissors
- Glue

This is an intuitive game for both children and adults. Cut out lots of pictures, images and letters from the comics and magazines. Once you have done this, ask everyone to stick them with glue wherever they want on their own box and lid. This creative box tells you about their personality: the lid of the box tells you about the person they are with others; the sides tell you about their characteristics; the inside of the box is what they hold special; the bottom of the box is what they keep to themselves. Once the box is finished, take turns at using your psychic powers to see what the box has revealed.

We are not usually encouraged to say how things make us feel or what impression we get of them. We are expected to conform to the 'norm', whatever that happens to be at the time. By playing these sorts of games, though, you are showing your child that you are happy to talk about feelings and that you do see the value in intuition. Not only will it give them the chance to show off a little bit, but they will be delighted that you are recognising and validating their skills.

The gift of intuition is lost by careless words with no thought behind them – phrases such as, 'You should know better, you're a big boy now,' or, 'Act your age,' or, 'Grow up, you're not a little girl any more.' Such things make me shudder. I bet we've all had at least one of them addressed to us in our lifetime, and may have used the words ourselves if we were careless.

It is important to use the correct language when dealing with children, especially highly sensitive ones. Just think how often you, as an adult, dwell on something your boss or work colleague has said to you. Think of how you pick apart what a friend *really* means by what she says about your new dress. And don't even get me started on the things you still remember *your* mother saying to you when you were a child that she forgot as soon as the words came out of her mouth! Now, if that is the case for an adult, what is it like for a child? And how much worse is it for an intuitive child? Words are wonderful and powerful, but that power can be dangerous and damaging too.

Your own talents

If you are reading this book because you think you had psychic gifts as a little one, I hope that I have, in some way, made you feel more positive about rekindling your latent talents. If you have tried the games above for yourself, you may be ready to progress. In order to do this, you may need to take leave of your ordinary senses and explore the next phase.

I've lost track of the number of times that I have told people about events that happened when they were a child and explained that they had a psychic ability which was later shelved or killed off. At one show, I spoke to a young woman who was about thirty years old. I told her that her work was at a critical juncture and that things were very uncertain. She agreed. I said that she had always wanted to get into nursing, but that she had put that on the back burner and fallen into an office job instead. I then observed that her father had been trying to contact her and that she had felt his energy. Again, she agreed, but was very nervous when I brought this up. I knew that she was afraid to let him communicate in case it reopened the floodgates and took her back to her childhood when she saw spirit clearly.

She was extremely emotional, but said that it was all true. I told her that there had been a time when she needed to shut off from the gift because she didn't fully understand it and was afraid, but that now was the time to reconnect with spirit. Her father had come forward to make it easy for her. He was to be her guide and assist her progress. Often someone close will come to help make the transition an easy one, as in this case, but this can only happen if the person is ready to accept it. A psychic light that has been extinguished can always be rekindled.

Alistair's journey

Once when I did a show in Rochdale, I was approached by a spirit who wanted to talk with a man called Alistair who was in the audience. Alistair was a real cynic – he had been brought along by his sister, and was there under duress from what I could see. This makes no difference to spirit, though. If they want to make contact, they will. I am just the conduit for that moment and they don't particularly care if I'm going to find it difficult or awkward to make someone believe. It's as if they are standing with a letter that they need to deliver and they will keep knocking and knocking at the door until someone answers.

I identified Alistair through what his grandfather told me, but his body language and face were screaming that he didn't want to hear anything. To begin with, I didn't mention that I was communicating with his grandfather, just that I had someone in spirit. When I did finally release that bit of information, Alistair opened up slightly and sat up in his seat paying more attention. They had been very close and I was able to remind him of the many hill-walking outings they used to enjoy and the adventures they had together. Alistair nodded his head throughout, so I was sure that he was listening to me.

I told Alistair that I was fully aware that he was a non-believer, but that I also knew he'd had an experience in his life which he simply could not explain. He looked very puzzled at that – and I knew that this wasn't because he didn't know what I was referring to but because he couldn't understand how I could possibly have known about it. He started to look very uncomfortable and was shifting about in his seat, mumbling that he wasn't sure what I was saying.

I told him in no uncertain terms that he knew exactly what I was talking about because his grandfather was relaying all of the information to me. 'This all happened when your grandfather was still on the Earth plane. You were woken up one night in bed and had a feeling that something had happened. You kept hearing your grand-father's name in your head as if someone was telling you to go and see him. You got dressed in the middle of the night and went to his house. When you arrived, the old man was lying on the floor, having been taken very ill. You called an ambulance and your grandfather was saved, thanks to your intervention, and the intervention of whoever was calling on you that night.'

As I recounted the story, Alistair was in floods of tears. His grandfather lived a good few years after the stroke that had affected him that night, thanks to Alistair acting on something he could never explain. The old man was now trying to connect through me as he had been unable to get his grandson to recognise any of the messages he sent directly. He wanted Alistair to know that the cyni-cism he had tried to cultivate was wrong, that he had a talent and that he had experienced spirit for himself. Now was the time for him to develop his gift and to accept the many messages he was being sent.

Some years later, when I was back in Rochdale, I went to a local spiritualist church. To my absolute surprise and delight, Alistair was there. He had joined a development circle to assist his gift. He thanked me for turning his life around and for helping him to continue his relationship with his grandfather.

Sometimes it is the role of a child who has passed over to help someone left behind regain their psychic potential; they become their spirit guide. This happens frequently between siblings, because the remarkable bonds they forge with each other in childhood keep them connected despite the death of one of them. Erin, a young woman in her early twenties, came to me for a reading. She said that she was interested in hearing about the usual things – work and romance – but as soon as I began I sensed the presence of a child. Erin confirmed that she often felt the presence of this child, whom I correctly identified as her little brother.

I told Erin that he would assist her on her path through life, and keep her on the right one. I knew that Erin had always been very psychic, but that she was a bit scared of her gift. Her brother was there to tell her that using it was the right thing to do and that she should take it forward. He would be her guide for as long as she needed him, but I told her that need may change as she developed. Her brother was giving her the biggest gift he could – and continued to show how much he loved her from the other side by being her spirit guide.

These stories are just some of many about people I've encountered who have had psychic gifts from childhood, but who have ignored or dismissed them. Often, it is only with the help of someone who loves them on the other side that they can reconnect to their childhood talents and be the person they are meant to be.

Changing your belief system to find
a new way forward

In the scheme of things, if you believe that you are co-creator with your higher self, the universe or higher consciousness, then that gives you carte blanche to create your new senses. These words may not be clear to you now, but remember the analogy that this is a new language in a new country for you, a country where I've been going on my holidays for a while! In more simple terms, the first step to this is to change your underlying belief system that tells you it's impossible or that only certain people have 'the gift' to be telepathic, telekinetic, a seer, in touch with the angels, a healer or anything else that you can imagine. If you begin to change your beliefs around this and, as a result, your thought patterns, change will happen. You will open the door to a world of possibilities. These possibilities mean that you can create whatever you want. Imagine your own personal genie, one that provides your every wish – it's yours for the taking. Once you begin this journey your ordinary senses will still be there, but they will be heightened as a result of your higher development and new-found talents. When you connect with spirit and have started on the path to psychic development, then you will see more clearly, hear more sharply, feel more intensely and just know in your gut and your heart that you are right. You will also know it in your soul, and I believe that is another area which we often neglect.

The ultimate purpose of the journey made by the soul is not about the wealth, property or possessions we acquire, but about the experience we gain along the way. It's about how we overcome the obstacles in life and what we learn from it all. The soul cannot take with it material possessions as we know them, but it can take all the wealth of knowledge and skills learned along the way. This will all be put to use at some point in the future if we choose to reincarnate into another life (see p. 72).

We can get hung up on thinking that by a certain age we need to have bought a house, had children, seen the world or be settled in a secure job. And we feel that if we have not, we have failed. But these effects do not feed your soul if you are acquiring them for the sake of it. Children are wonderful, if you become a parent for the right reason; a successful career can give so much to others, but the accumulation of money alone is meaningless in the grand scheme of things. This is not what 'it' is all about, and we will end up full of guilt and resentment if we focus on the wrong things – on the accessories, rather than the core.

If we were to take the view that everything is experiential, we would not tie ourselves in such knots, and it would at the very least release us from the emotional wrangles that we put ourselves through. It may be an interesting concept to think about each situation that comes up and pose the question: Why does my soul need this experience? What will my soul gain from it? All at once, life becomes much more exciting and an adventure once you remove the superficial materialism.

Now I know that belief systems are instilled in us from a very tender age, and that all of this is easier said than done; however, if you work at it – like anything else – you will soon be able to adopt it as a new way in which to function.

The soul's expression through the physical body while in this incarnation is to want to touch, taste, smell, feel, intuit and experience as much as it can. We are all very gifted or talented in one way or another and there are those who are simply geniuses from the moment they are born – gurus and masters at what they do. This must have come from somewhere even though they may not remember exactly where. When you think about the souls who arrive here with psychic and intuitive gifts, they are no different from anyone else; perhaps they have a need at some level to experience what it would be like to be this way and what they will gain in knowledge from it.

Trust is the key to believing in your own abilities, otherwise the questions will remain. If we are here to live out some requirement for our soul, then we must make that our reality. And I think that adopting this attitude will make a massive difference when our time comes to move on to the afterlife. That afterlife is nothing more than another step in the soul's movement to continue to experience at another level. The soul in its essence is linked to the greater consciousness. It is part of everything and everything is part of it. We are here and everywhere all at once, and if we can lift our vibration high enough then we will be able to tap into that powerful consciousness.

Clairvoyants and mediums are able to tap into the energy of those who have passed on by linking with their energy at a certain level. We can even get messages from souls who have reincarnated by tapping into their energy as they were, because the information is held in the greater consciousness, the greater cosmic soul.

Do you want to ensure that the growth of your soul is aligned with your gift? Do you want to be who you came here to be? If so, now is the time to look deeper at how you bring about your desires. I would say that it will depend very much on where your soul is in its evolution; what it needs, it will create. Understanding that if *you* wanted to change things in *your* world *you* could certainly won't do you any harm.

I would love all children to have access to that way of thinking – to have the space to grow and reach their potential. I didn't have the best of upbringings, but it was actually a gift because it made me who I am.

My daughter recently asked me, 'When are you going to stop?'

I asked her what she meant, and she said, 'You're always looking to the next thing, moving on to the next stage, wondering what you can try and do.'

I thought about this and realised quite quickly why I am this way. It's because I'm always trying to prove to myself that I'm all right. Throughout my own childhood my home environment was very cold, a very practical household, and I felt I was a second-class citizen – mostly in the eyes of my dad. He had a connection with my sister, so I knew he was capable of it, but I just didn't know what had happened in my dad's life to make him unable to connect with me. I was never told I was good at anything, so I never thought I'd amount to much. My mum always said I was highly strung, but I now know that this applies to all intuitive children.

So I have always needed to prove that I can do something, that I'm not stupid and, as my daughter has noticed, I'm always trying to achieve. I've done courses in chemistry and in bioscience; I've done so many things that my parents would never have expected of me – but it's all about reassuring myself. If my parents had recognised that, they could have done so much more to encourage my talents and help me to blossom.

If you can help any child, please do. If you have a child who is very shy and timorous and terrified of everything

– as I was – then you have a responsibility to ensure that child does not lead an empty existence. I'm at peace with my past now, as it was one of the things which made me stronger, but I hate to think of anyone else going through that same process. The psychic child can make a huge difference to the world – and you can make a huge difference to theirs.

Thank you

There have been times when I've had enough of this plane. There have been times when I've said this to my family and told them that it's time for me to go home. Sometimes I can't wait. There will be peace. I hope I retain a memory of my time here but I am ready for it to end.

When I think of all that I have seen and all that I have been a part of, I know that I have been blessed. I have been given so much by my wonderful family, and, as if that wasn't enough, I've had all of *this* on top. It is such a privilege to be able to hear people's stories and to help bring comfort to those who have lost loved ones. I guess what I'm saying is that I know just how hard life can be, but I also know how beautiful it is too.

I would love for everyone to take three things from this book:

Firstly, treasure every moment you have. Grab on to each bit of love and give even more of it away. Your heart has the capacity to hold and to share enormous amounts of it, so don't be shy. Even if this isn't your first or last time on this plane, you will be selling yourself short if you don't make the most of it.

Secondly, as someone once said, 'Don't sweat the small stuff.' If this book has taught you anything, it should be that we are all part of a much bigger picture. Getting stressed about having the right shoes for a party, whether you've missed your favourite TV programme or the fact that your next-door neighbour has parked in 'your' space again isn't terribly important in the grand scheme of things, so let all of the nonsense go. What you will be left with is a calmer approach to life and more opportunity to concentrate on the important things. Take comfort in what there is and don't worry about what there is not.

Thirdly, encourage, love and respect the psychic children who are all around us. They could change this world if only we allowed their talent to shine and started to realise that we are all capable of so much more. Look at every baby and every toddler and every child in your family or network in a new way – the light that shines within them could teach you so much if you opened your eyes, mind and heart. Let's all glory in the wonder of the many psychic children around us. Through accepting and encouraging their gifts we can all make this plane a better place.

It has been a pleasure to share my stories with you. I would be delighted if you would like to share some with me, and you can contact me through my website (www.

joancharles.co.uk), my publisher (www.harpercollins.
co.uk), my agent (Clare Hulton) or my ghostwriter
(www.lindawatsonbrown.co.uk). Until we meet again,
when I will tell you more of my tales of the other side,
love yourself and forgive yourself. It's all part of an aston-
ishing journey.

Joan

Acknowledgements

On this spiritual journey I have been fortunate enough to be surrounded by many lovely souls who have inspired and supported me. The individuals I have had the pleasure of meeting at my shows and those who are or have been clients have all taught me something special along the way.

I want to give a special thank you to Linda Watson Brown, whom I have had the pleasure of knowing for many years – she is an inspiration, dedicated, and a truly spiritual soul. Her amazing talents have brought my book to life beautifully and totally without any ego. Our agent, Clare Hulton, has given us her exceptional expertise and understanding, and brought this whole project together, and Vicky McGeown at HarperCollins has made it easy for me to turn my dream into a reality.

I have spoken a lot about two of my grandchildren and my girls – this in no way reflects how I feel about the rest of the wee angels and my two sons. I love them all very dearly; it's just that the stories I have written about have come from Dannielle, Simonne, Ellie and Colin.

The vast majority of names have been changed in the book as these stories are very personal, but there are some friends who do deserve 'public' credit – namely, Victoria Lynn Weston, Penney Pierce, Paul Von Ward, Cynthia Sue Larson, Dr Francesca McCartney and Arupa Tesolin.

I would also like to thank Patricia Kane for being such a help and support to me in the early days – a true friend.

In acknowledging what has brought me here, I cannot leave out one of the most crucial elements. The spirit world has never let me down and continues to amaze me with the information brought forward to loved ones on the Earth plane – I would not be writing this book if it were not for their continual presence in my life. This is as much a dedication to them as it is an acknowledgement. Thank you all from the bottom of my heart.